360°
Feedback

360°
Feedback

The Powerful New Model for Employee Assessment & Performance Improvement

Mark R. Edwards
and Ann J. Ewen

amacom
American Management Association

New York • Atlanta • Boston • Chicago • Kansas City • San Francisco • Washington, D.C
Brussels • Mexico City • Tokyo • Toronto

This publication is designed to provide accurate and authoritative
information in regard to the subject matter covered. It is sold with
the understanding that the publisher is not engaged in rendering
legal, accounting, or other professional service. If legal advice or
other expert assistance is required, the services of a competent
professional person should be sought.

Library of Congress Cataloging-in-Publication Data

Edwards, Mark R. (Mark Robert), 1949–
    360° feedback : the powerful new model for employee
assessment & performance Improvement / Mark R.
Edwards and Ann J. Ewen.
      p. cm.
    Includes bibliographical references and index.
    ISBN 0-8144-0326-3
    1. Employees—Rating of.   2. Performance—Evaluation.
    I. Ewen, Ann J.
HF5549.5.R3E33   1996
668.3'125—dc20   96-6098
                                         CIP

Printing number

10 9 8 7 6 5 4

Contents

Acknowledgments

The authors would like to thank the many innovators who in the 1970s and 1980s were willing to test 360° feedback systems before they became popular. Special thanks go to Adrienne Hickey, Theresa Plunkett, and Richard Gatjens at AMACOM; development editor, Jacqueline Laks Gorman; our editorial assistant, Jeni Servo; and our production team, Karen Bruggeman and Mari Phipps.

Part I

The New Assessment Model

1

The Power of
360° Feedback

Any company that's going to make it in the 1990s and beyond has got to find a way to engage the mind of every single employee. If you're not thinking all the time about making every person more valuable, you don't have a chance. What's the alternative? Wasted minds? Uninvolved people? A labor force that's angry or bored? That doesn't make sense.

—John F. Welch, Jr., CEO, GE

No one would have doubted his ability to reign had he never been emperor.

—Tacitus, Roman historian

THE EMPEROR'S NEW CLOTHES:
AN UPDATED LEADERSHIP TALE

Once upon a time, the Emperor asked members of his court how he looked in his new clothes. Knowing the answer he wanted, his courtiers told him "superb," in spite of the fact that he had on not a stitch of clothing.

The Emperor had just read about how people often tell others to their face what they *want* to hear rather than what they *need* to hear. The Emperor was anxious because he had scheduled a large parade, and would be wearing his new clothes in it. At the last moment, he asked those in his circle of influence—those he most trusted—to provide him *anonymous* feedback about the look of his new suit. The anonymous feedback was unanimous: He was wearing only his birthday suit.

The Emperor used what is today called 360° feedback to overcome false information. Imagine how many kings, queens, presidents, generals, leaders, and individuals have been influenced by information gathered in a manner that reinforced their false assumptions rather than told the truth. The honest input from others can overcome false self-perceptions, blind spots, and just plain ignorance. Candid feedback from relevant others may save careers when people can avoid making stupid mistakes (like parading naked in public).

A New Model for Performance Feedback and Appraisal

Like the Emperor, leaders and employees at all levels of organizations are changing the way they receive feedback in order to improve the quality of information. The new model for performance feedback and appraisal turns the assessment process upside down. People are asking for performance feedback from those in their own circle of influence, that is, those with knowledge of their work behaviors, as well as from their supervisor. This information that comes from many asking for and getting information from people rather than just is more honest, reliable, and valid than traditional appraisals from the supervisor only. Moreover, feedback from these multiple sources has a more powerful impact on people than information from a single source, such as a supervisor. In fact, *no organizational action has more power for motivating employee behavior change than feedback from credible work associates.*

The 360° feedback® process, also called multisource assessment, taps the collective wisdom of those who work most closely with the employee: supervisor, colleagues (peers), direct reports (subordinates), and possibly internal and often external customers.* The collective intelligence these people provide on critical

*360° feedback® is a registered trademark of TEAMS, Inc.

competencies or specific behaviors and skills gives the employee a clear understanding of personal strengths and areas ripe for development. Employees also view this performance information from multiple perspectives as fair, accurate, credible, and motivating. Employees are often more strongly motivated to change their work behaviors to attain the esteem of their coworkers than to win the respect of their supervisor alone.

As the 360° Feedback Process better serves the needs of employees, it serves the changing needs of their organizations too. Organizations are reducing hierarchy by removing layers of management and putting more emphasis on empowerment, teamwork, continuous learning, individual development, and self-responsibility. The 360° Feedback Model aligns with these organizational goals to create opportunities for personal and career development and for aligning individual performance expectations with corporate values.

Well-designed 360° feedback systems serve the many needs of employees substantially better than the traditional hierarchical, single-source assessments employees are so familiar with, such as management by objectives or results-only measures. Change agents, line and staff managers, team members, and employees in all disciplines are designing and implementing multisource assessment systems that work for people in nearly all kinds of jobs: nurses, lawyers, production workers, union members, hospitality personnel, engineers, military units, school teachers, librarians, research and development managers, and public safety officers, among many others. Any employee who needs better performance information may ask for and even implement a 360° feedback process.

Single-source assessments reinforce employee accountability and service to that single source, typically the boss. In contrast, multisource assessment creates accountability and service to all stakeholders: supervisor, external customers, and internal customers, including coworkers and direct reports.

This book offers a framework for understanding, designing, implementing, and evaluating the 360° Feedback Process. It also shows how organizations can build effective systems that support people and encourage their continued improvement.

What Is 360° Feedback and How Does It Work?

The 360° feedback model differs substantially from the traditional single-source assessment completed by the supervisor. Supervisor-only appraisal typically occurs once a year with the express purpose of providing employees with an assessment of their work performance and management with information it needs for decisions on pay and promotions. Unfortunately, the intent behind supervisory appraisals has not matched the results.

Not a Single-Source Performance Assessment

Supervisory appraisals are generally time-consuming, and typically both those who give them and those who receive them dislike them. Moreover, they usually don't work; they neither differentiate levels of performance nor motivate employees to improve performance.

Supervisors tend to dislike appraisals so much they often avoid doing them completely or put them off as long as possible. A supervisor may report giving appraisals "on an ongoing basis," but his or her employees often cannot remember receiving a performance review. Some organizations have even reported employees' refusing promotions to supervisor because they did not want to take on the responsibility of "playing God" during the appraisal process.

The supervisor-only performance assessment obviously relies on a single perspective: the supervisor's judgment. These performance measures tend to provide flat, nonspecific information about an employee's performance, and they have other problems as well:

- They may reflect self-serving and other individual biases.
- Politics, favoritism, and friendship may enter into the assessment.
- The supervisor may have had an insufficient opportunity or motivation to observe employee performance.
- The supervisor may be unwilling to confront poor performance.

• Different supervisors have degrees of rigor in making evaluation decisions.

Hence, an employee's supervisor-only performance appraisal may not truly reflect the individual's actual job performance. High-performing employees may receive poor appraisals that limit their opportunity for rewards such as pay increases and promotions due to the idiosyncrasies of the supervisor. Most people can relate examples of employees who have had their career lives shattered by a single, possibly biased, supervisor.

Improving the Performance Picture

By increasing the number of evaluations to offer a more balanced and comprehensive view, the 360° feedback process improves the quality of performance measures. Because the feedback providers are those with whom the employee interacts regularly at work, their assessments are reliable, valid, and credible. This knowledge network of coworkers, who have firsthand experience with the employee, offers insight about work behaviors that a supervisor may not be able to observe. The 360° feedback process and traditional single-source, supervisor-only assessment are illustrated in Figure 1-1.

What Are the Benefits of 360° Feedback?

Organizations that adopt 360° feedback want better performance information and seek to motivate behavior change. They may have other purposes in mind too: to support a cultural change, reinforce team behaviors, or implement strategic initiatives, such as total quality management.

Most commonly, 360° feedback serves as a supplement to, not a replacement for, supervisory review. It blends the multisource feedback on behaviors or competencies with the supervisor's assessment of results. Individuals are evaluated both on how they do the job—that is, their behaviors—and what they do—their results or outcomes.

Figure 1-1. Single-source versus multisource feedback systems.

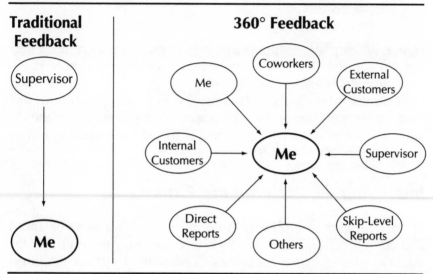

Benefits to Key Stakeholders

The 360° feedback process offers extensive and diverse benefits to key stakeholders in the organization—and the organization too:

- *Customers.* The process gives customers a chance to strengthen the customer-supplier relationship. The 360° feedback captures the relevant and motivating information from internal and external customers while giving them a voice in the assessment process.
- *Employees.* By participating in a process that has tremendous impact on their careers, employees may help select what evaluation criteria will be used to judge their performance and who will provide feedback. Participation plays a critical role for employees as they determine the fairness of the process.
- *Team members.* The only option for identifying team and individual members' effectiveness is 360° feedback. Failing feedback from multiple sources, team members lack the information necessary for effective individual development

and teamwork. With no team evaluation, accountability may evaporate, and performance may falter.

- *Supervisors.* This process expands supervisors' insight regarding the performance of each direct report by providing them more comprehensive and detailed performance information than they usually have access to. Also, the process typically reduces by half, or more, the supervisor's time spent on evaluating individual employees—a necessity as spans of supervision increase and work loads become heavier.

- *Leaders and managers.* The process provides leaders and managers an opportunity to tap information from the organization that may otherwise not be shared with them for fear of reprisal. Employees may identify areas of concern and suggestions for improvement, which leaders can use to guide the organization more effectively.

- *Organizations.* Organizations can gain access to credible, quantitative information to understand organizational strengths and weaknesses, leadership gaps, and training needs more fully. This information is much more useful than relying on intuitive judgment or responding to those who are making the most noise.

Figure 1-2 highlights the benefits to these stakeholders.

Who Is Using 360° Feedback?

Both public and private sector organizations are adopting 360° feedback systems. Recent survey research suggests that more than 90 percent of the Fortune 1000 companies use some form of multisource assessment system for at least developmental feedback. The innovators in 360° feedback include the U.S. Department of Energy, Disney, Arizona State University, Monsanto, Florida Power & Light, du Pont, Westinghouse, Motorola, Federal Express, Kino Hospital, Fidelity Bank, and McDonnell-Douglas.

Organizations with unions are also adopting multisource systems but not as quickly as companies without unions. Some union leaders do not support systems whereby members provide evalua-

Figure 1-2.   360° feedback benefits to key stakeholders.

Customers	*Supervisors*
• Input to service	• An opportunity to see a mirror
• A voice in the service process	of personal supervisory skills
• Participation in product and	• High-quality information for
service decisions	selection decisions
• A presence in the quality	• A change in role from
control process	performance judge to coach
• An opportunity to reward and	• Credible information to
recognize quality	confront poor performance
• An opportunity to contribute	• Credible information about
new ideas	behaviors that may derail a
	career

Employees	*Leaders*
• A voice in decision processes	• An opportunity to see how they
that most affect them (e.g.,	are viewed by others
appraisal)	• High-quality information for
• An opportunity to influence	selection decisions
career development	• A change in role from
• More impact on decisions at all	performance judge to coach
levels	• Credible information to
• A voice in leadership quality	confront poor performance
control	• Work group or unit training and
• An opportunity to reward and	development needs
recognize quality	• Quality assessment of direct
	reports

Teams	*Organization*
• An opportunity to see how the	• Better human resources
team serves customers	decision information
• High-quality information for	• Enhanced quality control and
selecting team members	validity for promotions
• An opportunity to assess team	• Increased employee motivation
development needs	• An opportunity to link
• Credible information about	performance and rewards
team leadership	• An opportunity to align vision,
• Credible information about	values, and competencies
team member contribution	
• Relevant information on team	
performance	

tions of each other, because they worry that such information could be used for performance ratings or discipline. But other union leaders recognize that fairer and more accurate performance feedback is a benefit in work settings and realize that the 360° feedback process gives union members a voice in identifying management strengths and development needs. Direct, early communication with union leadership in developing a 360° feedback process is necessary to ease any fears.

How Is 360° Feedback Being Used?

Most organizations with 360° feedback use it primarily for employee development rather than to support appraisal and pay decisions. In this use, the behavior feedback goes only to the subject. When the supervisor sees the behavior feedback, it impacts the supervisor's perception of the employee's performance. Knowledge of how a person is seen by others may have significant positive or negative impact, especially when such information comes from credible work associates. Hence, the 360° feedback becomes part of the performance management process.

Why Are Organizations Adopting These Systems?

Structural and cultural factors and employee relations have motivated organizations to begin experimenting with 360° feedback systems. For example, as organizations remove layers of management, flatten their structure, and begin using self-directed teams, the only practical option for performance feedback is from multiple sources. As organizations change their culture to align with their vision and values, 360° feedback becomes an ideal choice to communicate the new competencies required by the new values. For example, as Intuit moves to work teams, feedback on competencies associated with teamwork support the new team-building culture. Also, employees ask for multisource assessment to get a more balanced view of their performance from the various perspectives.

Structural Changes

Organizational structures have changed substantially since the mid-1980s. The 360° feedback process offers support for these structural changes, such as growth in supervisors' spans of control, the increased use of technical or knowledge workers, the introduction of matrix and project management organization design, and the move to working in teams. The following sections look at a number of reasons that organizations have introduced multisource assessment.

Increased Spans of Control

A typical manager used to supervise three to nine employees. Today, Intel, Bausch & Lomb, Compaq Computers, American Express, Glaxo, Inc., and many other production and service companies have moved from traditional spans of control to one supervisor for as many as seventy or more direct reports. Classic supervisor-only evaluation systems are no longer practical because supervisors with a large number of reporting relationships lack the opportunity to observe many individual performance actions.

Knowledge Workers

A supervisor may not have enough technical or expert knowledge to provide credible performance feedback on employees in positions requiring highly specialized knowledge, like MIS managers or scientists. Many organizations, such as Lawrence Livermore National Laboratory, Intuit, Whirlpool, and Bellcore, have adopted a multisource system to provide accurate assessments by coworkers with similar expertise.

Matrix and Project Management

Many organizations, like Florida Power & Light, Salt River Project (a utility company), and Monsanto, have adopted 360° feedback systems because their employees work in matrix or project management situations, with employees often reporting to more than one supervisor during a project. Matrix organization structures occur as a result of the need to deploy human assets at high velocity. People move quickly from project to project and may only occasionally interact directly with their supervisor. Project management designs require information from multiple sources because no one person has sufficient information to provide a complete performance picture of the individual.

Teams

When the organizational structure has moved from classic supervisory designs to work teams, with leadership dispersed throughout the team, team members offer highly credible performance feedback. Among the organizations using 360° feedback systems for this reason are Motorola, Glaxo, General Motors Acceptance Corporation, Allied Signal, Digital, and Kino Hospital.

Changes in Organization Culture

Revolutionary changes in organization cultures also have made traditional single-source assessments illogical and impractical. Among these changes are increasing participative leadership, empowering employees, improving customer service, integrating quality initiatives into the mainstream of business activities, reengineering, moving to competency- and team-based rewards, and ending entitlements.

Participative Leadership

Current, Inc., BellSouth, Lotus Development, and AT&T have given employees a voice in organizational decision processes and have adopted 360° feedback systems to drive culture change and align individual behaviors with organizational values and objectives. Leaders who best empower employees are recognized and rewarded when those they lead provide excellent performance feedback.

Empowerment

American Airlines, Coca-Cola, and General Electric have driven decision making down to the lowest possible level. Bob Crandall, CEO of American Airlines, points out that behavior feedback from multiple sources encourages every employee to take actions aligned with the new organizational culture. He observes that "what you measure is what you get." The 360° feedback process communicates the appropriate actions needed from employees to support this cultural change, and these actions are then recognized and rewarded.

Customer Service

Federal Express, Chemetals, Maricopa Colleges, Monsanto and Mesa (Arizona) Schools have used the 360° feedback process to gather and act on information from both internal and external customers. The improved communication that results can translate to better customer service.

Quality Focus

The cultures at McDonnell-Douglas, Samaritan Health Systems, and SunQuest Computers value data-based decisions as a result of their continuous quality improvement initiatives. The 360° feedback systems provide the best measures for competencies. This logical application for individual performance measurement meshes with the organization's quality philosophy.

Reengineering

Reengineering, or the reinvention of work processes, often requires new methods to obtain accurate performance measures. Reengineering actions focus on redesigning the way employees work in order to improve individual, team, and organizational productivity. Since 360° feedback systems improve the quality of information, these systems logically support the reengineering effort at organizations like Tenneco, Whirlpool, Lands' End, and Intuit.

Competency-Based Rewards

Monsanto, the U.S. Department of Energy, Westinghouse, and Hewlett-Packard have used 360° feedback systems to support new recognition and reward systems that focus on critical success factors or competencies—the knowledge, skills, abilities, and motives that differentiate high, medium, and low performers. Competencies have been called the DNA of organizations because they create a differential advantage for one organization compared with another. Organizational competencies, sometimes called core competencies, are those qualities that distinguish an organization's products or services from those of its competitors and establish value in the minds of its customers. Individual competencies may be thought of as the bundle of knowledge, skills, and abilities employees bring to their work.

Information from multiple sources offers the best method for measuring competencies. Traditional, single-source measures are deficient at assessing competencies because supervisors seldom have sufficient opportunity to observe each employee's full range of work behaviors.

Team-Based Rewards

Motorola, General Motors Acceptance Corporation, Gore Industries, and Lands' End reengineered parts of their organization into teams, none of them with a formal supervisor. 360° feedback systems are the most appropriate way to evaluate individual performance and contribution. Team assessment provides these organizations with a credible information source for recognition and rewards.

End of Entitlements

Multisource performance measures more clearly distinguish among levels of performance than do single-source measures. Many organizations find that single-source processes provide inflated evaluations, giving nearly everyone high performance ratings, and in the process creating an environment in which employees feel entitled to regular raises and promotions. Multisource assessments are substantially better at distinguishing high, medium, and low performers, enabling appropriate recognition and rewards and an end to automatic entitlements.

Employee Relations

No other information has more impact on an employee's career than information on his or her performance. Hence, the accuracy, fairness, and usefulness of performance measures are critical factors to employees. The 360° feedback process, which employees often design and introduce, improves employee relations by providing valid measures without bias toward minorities and women.

Career Development

Employees want honest feedback for their career development, yet managers, often finding it difficult to provide specific and critical feedback, tend to shy away from addressing performance problems.

The 360° feedback process yields specific and quantitative information for each employee to use in making intelligent career decisions. When work associates are assured that they will remain anonymous, they are willing to provide insight they might not reveal in a face-to-face meeting.

Fair Reward Decisions

Managers and employees want pay and promotion decisions to be fair. Research across large sets of employee groups indicate that users perceive 360° feedback to be more fair than single-rate processes. When these decisions occur in a culture where rewards are based on performance or contribution rather than on seniority or politics, they will be fair.

Accurate Performance Measures

Common sense, supported by compelling research, shows that assessment by multiple coworkers is more reliable and objective than information gained from a single person. The 360° feedback process collects information from those with the best knowledge of the individual's performance because they have the best opportunity to observe work behaviors.

Valid Performance Measures

An employee can discount a single-source assessment easily by invalidating the source. Employees commonly complain: "My supervisor is biased" or "What does my supervisor know?" When the same information is provided by the individual's work associates, the employee perceives the results as having far more credibility.

Nonperformance

Supervisors must document, justify, and confront nonperformance and more often than not avoid the entire subject. Surveys show consistently that supervisors do not deal effectively with performance problems.

Consider the challenge of an employee whose job performance is plummeting because of substance abuse. A supervisor has many reasons to avoid confronting the problem. For example, he or she must document the problem and come up with some form of remediation. Rather than take on what may be a massive effort, many supervisors elect to look the other way. Indeed, a supervisor may be the last to know that a particular employee has a problem because he or she may try to hide revealing behaviors.

Work associates who are part of 360° feedback systems are rarely reluctant to identify poor performance or nonperformance. Moreover, team members are not reluctant to give a coworker a nudge if he or she is not sufficiently contributing to the team's efforts or if he or she needs help.

Diversity Management

Single-source performance measures often are biased against older workers, women, and people of color. Preliminary research shows that multisource performance measures moderate adverse discrimination against older employees, presumably recognizing the greater experience level; are generally neutral to women; and are nearly impartial to ethnicity.

Legal Protection

When decisions are based on single-source evaluations, the organization may find itself in the position of defending the judgment of a single person. One person, no matter how fair, is subject to claims of bias or partiality. Multisource measures offer substantially stronger legal protection because the model combines multiple perspectives, resembling the jury system. The probability that multiple people rating independently all share the same bias is very low. In addition, a formalized 360° feedback process may offer substantial safeguards by demonstrating process fairness to individuals and to groups.

What Are the Approaches to 360° Feedback?

Just as there are many reasons that organizations implement 360° feedback, there are a wide variety of ways to design the process, both formal and informal.

Organizations often begin the evolution to multisource systems with informal models that simply encourage managers and employees to receive feedback from internal customers. Such informal systems move the organization closer to true 360° feedback systems. In this process, employees typically recognize that the feedback that comes from a number of people contains substantial error because there are no process safeguards such as respondent anonymity and there may be unintentional or intentional respondent biases. Experience shows that the 360° feedback process must be formalized to ensure fairness and accuracy.

Informal Systems

Low-structure or informal multisource assessment models introduce people to the concept of receiving feedback from a number of people. These models are easy and fast to implement and offer a satisfactory initial exposure to multisource processes for the purpose of employee development. However, these quickly developed systems generally fail to provide sufficient safeguards to ensure fairness, and so they are likely to be insufficient for performance appraisal.

Many organizations assume that increasing the assessment pool beyond one person will improve the accuracy of measurement. It does not. In fact, *simplistic, informal approaches to multisource assessment are likely to multiply rather than reduce error.* Errors enter from respondents' concerns about anonymity and factors such as friendship, competition bias, and collusion. (Chapter 6 examines the necessary safeguards to ensure that the multiple sources provide high-quality assessments rather than multiplying error.)

The dangers of informal multisource systems are that they may:

- Report false information that appears credible ("How could all these people I trust be wrong?")
- Inappropriately impact an employee's self-perception (Employees may not recognize multisource assessment information that is false.)
- Inappropriately impact an employee's career (Employees may feel that false assessment information that is "only" developmental indicates that they do not have a chance for success as an organizational leader.)
- Negatively influence employees' willingness to participate in a fair and formalized or structured 360° feedback system (After seeing a process fail, users may be reluctant to even try a formalized process with safeguards.)

Organizations adopt multisource systems with the intent of improving information quality and reducing measurement errors. Informal multisource systems, while useful for individual employee development, may simply replace one set of assessment errors—from the supervisor—with others.

Formal Systems

A formalized 360° feedback system provides safeguards to ensure data integrity of the performance measures. It follows policy guidelines that address predictable user concerns, such as fairness in data collection, respondent anonymity, the method of scoring, and how the information is used. Formal structures take more time to design and implement and are more expensive because of the technology they use and the training they must provide. Nonetheless, sophisticated or formalized multisource assessment systems are recommended when feedback can affect an employee's career, such as when it is used in a performance review or to make a decision about a raise.

What Features Are Required for an Effective Process?

The intent of 360° feedback systems is to support people and encourage their continued improvement through the use of high-quality information. An effective 360° feedback process may include input from one set of employees, such as only direct reports, or multiple sets of sources, such as colleagues or direct reports. This process:

- Allows the process design to be created by those who use the system—employees and managers.
- Uses a valid process for developing employees' competencies for assessment.
- Uses a valid method for selecting evaluation teams, with a minimum of four respondents in addition to the supervisor and the person receiving feedback.
- Ensures absolute respondent anonymity and confidentiality for the feedback.
- Relies on a research-based protocol for collecting and scoring data and reporting information.
- Ensures that all participants are trained to provide and receive feedback.
- Includes an understandable process and technology safeguards to ensure fairness that is communicated to all participants.
- Is assessed for effectiveness, fairness, accuracy, and validity by the users.

- Includes an appeals procedure.

This list excludes a number of common features associated with informal systems:

- Simply getting feedback using a low-structure process like walking around and talking to people. Good managers have always gathered intelligence verbally from those around them.
- Second-level supervisory review of first-level assessments. Second-level supervisors seldom change or have reason to change the immediate supervisor's evaluation because they usually lack sufficient contact with the employee.
- Verbal discussions in which feedback providers are asked for their opinion individually or in a group. This model lacks respondent anonymity.
- Any process where respondent anonymity is not protected.
- Simple spreadsheet, survey, or other scoring processes that ignore and blindly score obviously invalid respondents.
- Off-the-shelf or externally validated surveys if there are insufficient safeguards to ensure user fairness such as respondent accountability and specific job relevancy to the organization.

What Differentiates This 360° Feedback Approach?

There is no commonly accepted model or standardized approach to 360° feedback systems. You may find that some of the recommendations we make are contrary to prevailing current practice because many organizations have experience only with informal systems. Many informal systems reflect one of the following conditions:

- Single-rater (self or supervisory) assessments are extended to multisource settings.
- Traditional survey models, where sample sizes of fifty or more are assumed, are inappropriately extended to small

sample conditions associated with 360° feedback, where evaluation team sizes are very small.

Systems that make these mistakes are prone to fail. Moreover, organizations that use these flawed systems are likely to have difficulty adopting multisource systems because they increase rather than reduce error. Many people have observed that they had to "unlearn" what they knew about both traditional single-source assessments and surveys in order to create effective 360° feedback systems.

Every element of the model we advocate in this book is based on field research and engineered to be used with the small respondent samples—often four to eight people—required for 360° feedback. The 360° feedback process we describe uses:

- Short surveys, which avoid respondent fatigue.
- A wider rating scale, such as 10 points, which creates richer, more specific feedback than the traditional 5-point scale.
- Intelligent scoring, which uses scientific methods to remove the influence of obviously invalid respondents, in order to reflect the collective intent of the multiple respondents.
- Process and technology safeguards, designed to reduce errors and enhance process fairness.

These and other issues unique to the specialized context of 360° feedback are addressed in this book as design issues in Chapters 4, 5, and 6.

The Structure of This Book

The 360° feedback process is not new. The process and research we describe here reflects our learnings from more than twenty years of experience and field research. Yet 360° feedback is new for many people in all types of industries who are evaluating and implementing multisource assessment processes for the first time. They recognize the potential power of the approach in increasing accuracy and fairness of performance feedback and appraisal. The book is designed to help users at all levels understand the process so that they can design and implement their own 360° feedback process.

Chapters 2 and 3 offer an overview of the background, approaches to, and illustrative applications for 360° feedback systems. To begin the process of building a 360° feedback system immediately, go directly to Chapters 4, 5, and 6. Chapter 7 explores predictable pitfalls, and common criticisms of the process are reviewed in Chapter 8. Chapter 9 examines the promise of 360° feedback systems in terms of measurable impacts on organizations, such as improvements in customer service measures and the positive results on diversity management. Chapter 10 offers insight into the future of intelligent 360° feedback systems.

2

360° Feedback Evolution and Variations

If you want one year of prosperity, grow grain.
If you want ten years of prosperity, grown trees.
If you want one hundred years of prosperity, grow people.
—Chinese Proverb

Lech Walesa told Congress that there is a declining world
market for words. He's right. The only thing the world
believes any more is behavior, because we all see it
instantaneously. None of us may preach anymore. We
must behave.

—Max DuPree, Chairman, Herman Miller

Variations of multisource systems have been in use for centuries.
When Julius Caesar's soldiers' lives were on the line, they decided
among themselves who would lead their unit into battle. If their
leader was struck down in the fighting, they would decide who
next would have the honor of leading them. Multiple assessors
(in the form of family members) have been used to support, or
recommend against, marriages every time a potential spouse has
been brought home to meet mom and dad. Multiple assessors are
commonly used to select the winner in beauty contests, choose
which vendor will win a contract, and determine who will hold
first chair in symphonies. Every major sports team uses a brain-
trust of coaches, and sometimes players, to make strategic decisions during games. Many businesses already use multiple source
assessments among the board of directors and top management
for important strategic decisions. Much in the same way, business

organizations are adapting this broadly accepted societal process to their employee development and performance assessment procedures.

We coined the term *360° feedback* in the mid 1980s based on user surveys and focus group analysis of what were then called multirater systems. We found that many people did not like the term *rater* and also confused *multirater* with *multiraiders* (as in the popular movie *Raiders of the Lost Ark*).

TEAMS, Inc. (our consulting firm) selected and registered 360° feedback as a trademark to represent its proprietary multisource process that includes process and technology safeguards, such as intelligent scoring and reporting. We used *360° feedback* in national and international advertising and training materials for several years before it was picked up by the *Wall Street Journal* in 1993 to describe feedback from multiple sources for development purposes. Soon after, *Fortune* quoted Jack Welch, CEO of General Electric, saying he used 360° feedback for all his executives because it was such a tough assessment. Almost instantly, the term became very popular to describe almost any procedure that collected information from multiple sources.

Evolution of 360° Feedback

360° feedback systems evolved from organization surveys, total quality management, developmental feedback, and performance appraisals (Figure 2-1). Each line of practice has contributed to developing 360° feedback processes for organizations to use effectively in providing increased quantity and quality of information to individual workers.

Some organizations have adopted 360° feedback because it seems to be the logical next step from their current practice with organization surveys, a customer feedback process, or peer or upward appraisals. A few organizations—Monsanto, Tenneco, and du Pont, among them—were using all these lines of practice when 360° feedback was initiated, so many employees viewed the process more as an incremental development than a revolutionary change.

Figure 2-1. The roots of 360° feedback.

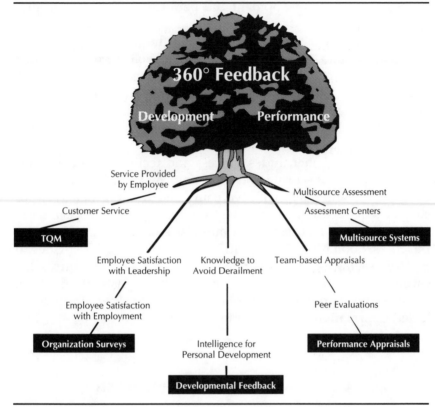

Organization Surveys

Organization surveys assess employee perceptions about work and the work setting. In the 1970s and 1980s, these surveys became more targeted and focused also on employees' satisfaction with their immediate leadership. As these surveys were scored in increasingly smaller groups, the scores became a surrogate measure of leadership quality. American Airlines, UPS, Houston Lighting & Power, and Whirlpool use these measures to recognize and reward effective leadership. The natural next step beyond departmental surveys is the use of surveys targeted specifically to the leader (*upward feedback* or appraisals) or to each employee (*multisource assessment*).

Total Quality Management (TQM)

The need to make data-driven decisions and improve information quality from customers and suppliers prompted an increase in the use of customer service surveys. These quality and customer service surveys, often designed as part of a TQM initiative, became more and more specific as customers responded first to the organization, then to a division, to a department, and eventually to their service representatives. Today, for example, most auto dealerships survey customers on their buying experience, asking for specific feedback on those with whom the customer directly interacted. Similarly, travelers commonly see "How did we do?" question cards in their hotel rooms, at their dinner table, and in rental cars. Even transportation firms asks for specific behavior feedback for drivers with, "How's my driving? Call 1–800-USA-SAFE."

Developmental Feedback

Feedback for the purpose of employee development became popular in the late 1980s. The concept of developmental-only feedback did not exist prior to the widespread use of multisource assessment. When supervisors alone provided evaluation, part of it was meant to be developmental, but employee surveys indicate that supervisory feedback often tends to focus on evaluative rather than developmental factors.

Developmental-only feedback helps employees avoid career derailment, which can occur when an employee's behaviors and work actions interfere with his or her career opportunities or promotions or may even lead to termination. Derailment may occur due to missteps in style, knowledge, skills, or abilities. For example, a supervisor who micromanages may find that less supervision of details creates more effective performance. An employee may be blind to or elect to ignore factors that may interfere with his or career success; work associates are typically quite willing to provide the needed insight.

As work environments and structures change, organizations are realizing the need for a base of developmental support and accountability that extends beyond the supervisor. Coworker support in the form of peer coaching is an obvious choice.

Performance Appraisals

Performance appraisals began in the late 1800s as the industrial age mechanized production processes. The age also led to a view of "man as machine" and the desire to increase individual output. Initial supervisory-only appraisals required supervisors to comment on subordinates. Later, they used trait checklists, which eventually evolved into various forms, scales, and behavioral descriptions designed to improve the quality of the singular judgment.

In the 1960s and 1970s, the management by objectives (MBO) approach, which compared individual results to organizational goals and strategies, became popular. These appraisals were provided by the supervisor but often encouraged employees to participate in developing work objectives and evaluate their own performance against the objectives they established. Changes in the workplace, such as flattened organization structures, teams, and changing employee expectations regarding their participation, helped organizations recognize multisource assessment as an appraisal alternative.

Leading management researchers—Ed Lawler, Richard Beatty, John Bernardin, Craig Schneier, Ken Wexley, and Gary Latham—recommend the use of multiple sources for performance appraisals, yet fewer than 6 percent of all organizations used multisource performance appraisals in 1995. Most organizations report that they have some form of 360° feedback but limit their use of this knowledge to employee development.

Peer Review

Peer reviews are distinctly different from the multisource assessment process of peer evaluation or appraisals and are *not* part of the evolutionary development of 360° feedback. They represent a step backward in the use of multisource assessment systems because the action associated with peer reviews is typically disciplinary. The bad name that peer reviews have due to their association with sanctions has seriously damaged the concept of peer appraisal, especially for positive actions such as development.

Multisource Assessment: A Brief History

All early multisource assessment applications were designed for performance management and appraisal. They required extensive administrative overhead and were too expensive to be considered sufficiently valuable for uses other than appraisal, pay, and promotion decisions. The concept of developmental-only feedback arose in the late 1980s, when standardized multisource assessments of leadership became popular.

1940s: Assessment Center

The assessment center, developed by British military intelligence in the early 1940s, was an early forerunner of a multisource assessment application. Multiple assessors reviewed participants' performance on tests, games, and simulations and then made collective judgments regarding the worthiness of candidates as foreign intelligence operatives. The industrial version, developed largely by Douglas Bray and associates at AT&T and enhanced by Bill Byham and associates at Development Dimensions, International, is still hailed as the most valid way to predict leadership success.

Assessment centers use a combination of assessments such as interviews and written and work activity tests that usually simulate an actual work setting. For example, an in-basket test, where assessees respond to a typical set of work-related memos and instructions, is scored according to how a candidate responds to worklike challenges. Scoring for other activities such as leaderless games is based on multiple assessors' observations of each candidate's actions and style. The assessment center's predictive validity comes from combination of multiple measures and multiple assessors.

360° feedback has been aptly described as an *in-situ,* or in-place, assessment center because the process provides highly credible and valid assessments in the actual job setting. In contrast to an assessment center, assessors in the 360° feedback process have firsthand knowledge of how each person responds at work because they work together. Although these two assessment processes are different in many ways, they share at their core a reliance on multiple independent judgments of human performance.

1950s and 1960s: Leadership Assessment and Selection

Military service academies have used multisource assessment for decades because research has shown these measures to be more valid for predicting leadership effectiveness than paper-and-pencil tests or fitness reports by officers. The first author worked on automating, using computer cards, the scoring for the multisource assessment process at the U.S. Naval Academy in the late 1960s. At Annapolis, all midshipmen are assessed by their classmates and commanding officers on their leadership skills. This process, called *peer grease*, has a significant impact on class standing and on what service assignments midshipmen can select when they graduate. Other military organizations, like U.S. Naval Air and the Israeli Air Force, have used multisource assessment for decades because it offers unique insight into the selection and development of pilots.

1960s: Job Evaluation

Commonly used multisource systems in the 1960s were job evaluation committees, hiring and internal selection panels, and promotional boards. The most popular job evaluation processes currently use a panel to review the relative value of jobs. A consensus among members of the job evaluation committee determines whether people get paid more for taking on additional responsibilities or performing more difficult jobs.

Tapping the collective wisdom of multiple respondents improves the quality and the credibility of selection decisions. The 360° feedback process imitates these processes using distributed respondents rather than a consistent evaluation panel.

1970s: Executive Selection

In the mid-1970s, organizations like Bank of America, Gulf Oil, United Airlines, and Kaiser Permanente created in-place reviews, with colleagues providing assessment of leadership effectiveness. These multisource assessments were used primarily for executive and management selection, now often called *succession planning*. Behavior profiles were costly and thus considered too expensive to use for developmental-only purposes for nonexecutive employees.

1970s: Project Evaluation and Placement

In the late 1970s, think tanks, such as those at Lawrence Livermore National Laboratories, Bell Labs, and G.A. Technologies, used multisource assessment to determine recognition, rewards, pay, placement, and promotion. Technical professionals immediately accepted the value of these assessments since they were scientifically accurate and predictably valid—but they insisted on setting up safeguards, including intelligent scoring, to compensate for the potential for unintentional and intentional biases.

1980s: Talent Assessment

In the early 1980s, organizations, including Disney, Federal Express, Westinghouse, Nestle, RCA, Ciba-Geigy, and Florida Power & Light, began experimenting with multisource assessment for leadership development, talent assessment, and performance appraisal. The corporate culture shifted to the belief that rewards, such as promotions, should be granted for performance as assessed by the individual's circle of influence rather than for currying the favor of a supervisor or as a right of tenure.

1980s: Performance Appraisal

In the mid-1980s, organizations like du Pont, Fidelity Bank, Arizona State University, Current, Inc., Midwestern Universities, and Monsanto began experimenting with multisource assessment for development and appraisal. These organizations had decided that multisource assessment was too expensive and time-consuming to use only for developmental purposes, so they supported the behavior feedback's being shared with supervisors to support, *but not replace*, supervisory decisions about performance and pay.

Why the Slow Adoption?

John Bernardin, who has probably written more on performance appraisal than any other author over the past twenty years, noted in 1985 that "every published report recommends multiple as opposed to single raters for performance appraisal."* If 360° feedback systems are so good, why have they been adopted so slowly? The answer lies in culture, inertia, budget, research, and technology.

Culture

Multisource assessment was considered counterculture until the benefits of total quality management systems became widely acknowledged. Receiving feedback from others with less experience, especially direct reports, was antithetical in American industry until only recently. Even today, some work cultures in America, and especially in South America, Asia, Indonesia, and India, discourage direct reports from providing leadership feedback. Similarly, superior officers in the military may see direct report feedback as inappropriate. Similarly, lawyers discount feedback from paralegal staff, doctors from nurses, pilots from flight crew, and professors from students.

Inertia

Most organizations are reluctant to change the way performance appraisals are conducted. A technology manager summarizes this feeling:

> "Changing to an informal 360° feedback process for development is like dieting. Changing to a formalized 360° feedback process to support appraisals is like changing bone structure."

Probably no other action is more central to an organization than the way performance is measured. Introducing multisource

---

*H. John Bernardin and Lawrence A. Klatt, "Managerial Appraisal Systems: Has Practice Caught Up With the State of the Art?" *Personnel Administrator,* vol. 30, no. 11 (November 1985), pp. 79–85.

assessment inverts the process because the power of the assessment process is now distributed throughout the organization.

Budget

Multisource systems require not just a budget but new money for a project administrator, a computer operator, training, and the resources to buy or create software to administer, score, and report the assessment information. Leaders repeatedly ask: "Why should we pay for something we already get for free?" But it is not free. Direct costs associated with single-source performance measures are nominal, yet the indirect cost required in managers' time to document and write appraisals is extensive. And there are opportunity costs too, which are associated with not having access to reliable and valid performance measures. These substantial indirect costs often are ignored when comparing single to multisource processes.

Research

Most of the published research on multisource systems has been conducted with small groups. While meta-analysis (studies of many studies) has provided compelling support for multisource assessment, very little research exists for issues such as how to implement, how to train for, and how to validate multisource assessment systems.

Technology

Mainframe computers supported multisource systems in the 1970s and 1980s; they were cumbersome, inflexible, slow, and expensive. Early PC applications were not much better. Better technology and software are now available, but organizations use equipment that varies substantially in capability.

Approaches to Multisource Assessment

During the 1970s and 1980s, organizations experimented with many variations of multisource assessment models, typically beginning with simple approaches, such as supervisors' informally gathering feedback from various sources. Eventually these systems evolved to more structured approaches with formal data collection, scoring, and reporting. The usual progression is as follows:

1. Appraisal by walking around (superior talks to supervisor).
2. Supervisor asks individuals for specific feedback.
3. Supervisor calls group meeting to discuss feedback.
4. Supervisor asks for written input from work associates.
5. Ratings are collated by secretary or specialist.
6. Ratings are scored using spreadsheet or surveys.
7. Work associates rate colleagues on disk.
8. Online assessment with safeguards.

Internally developed multisource assessment processes often encourage managers to solicit input from others, using any means available. Some managers simply talk to others; some ask for specific information. A surprisingly common response is to call a group meeting to discuss feedback about a particular person. These open sessions often lead to little real information and can cause very hard feelings.

One way supervisors seek to soften the aversive impacts from open feedback sessions is to ask for anonymous input from work associates. Yet user surveys consistently indicate that those who provide written feedback to supervisors do not feel their input is truly anonymous. And because this sort of information goes to the person being assessed or to the supervisor, work associates are understandably reluctant to be totally honest. They worry that the assessee will find out what they said.

The next level of feedback shifts the responsibility for administrating, collating, scoring, and reporting from the supervisor to a clerical person or other specialist, who is typically surprised at the substantial new workload he or she has been saddled with. Commonly, these administrators are not well trained and must find time for the multisource assessment scoring in addition to their existing jobs. Manual or semimanual tabulation processes are exceedingly tedious and subject to fatigue and scoring errors.

A specialist who supports the multisource process with scoring and reporting using a spreadsheet or a survey system overcomes many of the disadvantages of less sophisticated methods. Simplistic scoring methods are easy, cheap, and fast to implement. Survey and spreadsheet scoring systems could serve multisource assessments if the circumstances were the same as the large sample surveys for which these tools were designed. Unfortunately, 360° assessment uses sample sizes of only four to nine respondents, which makes them vastly different from traditional surveys. Therefore, spreadsheets and survey systems are likely to score obviously invalid responses, allowing respondent collusion and other actions that undermine the integrity of 360° feedback.

The use of specialized software that tracks respondents by name—yet maintaining their anonymity to the person receiving feedback—overcomes many of the problems with data integrity because invalid respondents can be identified and removed. Unfortunately, respondent tracking using paper surveys requires substantial administrative overhead; every survey must be unique because it represents a singular combination of subject and respondent. This administrative burden is beyond the acceptable limit for most organizations, so most have not created assessments that hold respondents accountable for the information they provide.

Automated systems, using either floppy disks or online input, enable multisource assessments to support a full range of safeguards without the substantial administrative overhead associated with paper surveys. Specialized software can be used to substitute technology for labor. For example, employees can select evaluation teams online and supervisors can approve the teams online, eliminating a large administrative task. The software can create all the relationships and automatically distribute electronic surveys, chalking up considerable savings in paper and administrative time.

The next level of sophistication in 360° feedback systems beyond the current online assessments with safeguards probably will be intelligent systems, discussed in Chapter 10.

Figure 2-2 summarizes the strengths and weaknesses of these methods.

Figure 2-2. Strengths and weaknesses of multisource assessment methods.

Style	Weaknesses	Strengths
Appraisal by walking around (supervisor talks to others)	May talk and not listen Low credibility Good managers have always done this	Easy and fast No cost
Supervisor asks for specific feedback from individuals	Very threatening Key people might not speak May undermine trust May upset employees Likely to create conflict and to demotivate employees due to the public discussion	Easy and fast No cost
Supervisor calls a group meeting to discuss feedback	Very threatening Key people might not speak May undermine trust May focus on negative Likely to demotivate employees due to public discussion	No explicit cost Easy and fast
Supervisor asks for "anonymous" written input from work associates	No respondent anonymity because employees feel the supervisor can identify their input Respondents might not be honest Does not work for upward feedback Not effective for narrative comments	Easy and fast for supervisor unless feedback must be compiled

Style	Weaknesses	Strengths
Ratings are collated by a secretary or specialist	Heavy burden on scorer Likely to create errors due to fatigue Not anonymous (the secretary sees the responses)	No outside cost Relatively easy for everyone but the scorer
Ratings are scored using spreadsheet or survey systems	Likely to multiply error due to the small samples and intentional respondent errors Heavy administrative burden if the surveys are tracked by respondent Few safeguards are available	Relatively fast and easy Low cost
Assessments occur on paper and are scored centrally or off-site	Requires specialized software Adds very high cost High administrative burden Most technology safeguards are difficult to use with paper surveys due to too much administrative overhead	Preserves anonymity Easy and fast for respondents
Online assessment with safeguards	Requires specialized software Adds to cost (substantially less expensive than papers surveys whether scored in-house or outsourced)	Preserves anonymity Easy and fast for respondents Enables many safeguards Four to six times more narrative comments as paper

Feedback Sources

The various approaches to multisource assessment also recognize the variety of feedback providers.

1° *Feedback: Self or Supervisor Assessment*

1° feedback typically comes from the supervisor, though sometimes from the employee or a second-level supervisor. These sources, which may provide input based on their singular perspective to multisource systems, have both strengths and weaknesses.

Self

Self-assessment often is used because it is an important comparison with other sources. Reliance on this form of assessment, however, may distort the accuracy of multisource measures. Self-ratings have been shown to be:

- Inflated due to self-serving bias (many people tend to have a higher opinion of themselves than do others).
- Inflated due to blind spots (lacking insight or knowledge, people tend to guess high).
- Adverse to women and nonwhites (in fact members of nearly every minority group tend to self-assess themselves lower than do the majority).

Research also demonstrates that some people are legends in their own minds. In a 360° feedback project that creates four levels of performance—low, medium, high, and very high—typically the lowest-performing group includes employees with the highest self-assessments.

A UNIVERSITY CONFRONTS A LOW-PERFORMANCE DEAN

The provost at a large university had a problem: One dean demanded substantial administrative time and resources. The provost repeatedly told the dean he was doing a poor job, while the dean repeatedly told the provost and the president that he was the best dean on campus. This stalemate continued for several years.

When the university adopted 360° feedback for all administrators and many faculty members, the dean was rated as the poorest-performing dean on campus. Not surprisingly, his self-rating was by far the highest among all deans. His response: "You asked the wrong people!"

During the next round, the dean selected multiple evaluation teams composed of faculty, dean's office staff, dean's advisory council members (external to the university), and students. Once again, and not surprisingly, all the different evaluation teams said the same thing: The dean was strong on research but poor on administrative action. All teams indicated that his failure to listen to others was derailing his career.

Fortunately, the dean was trained in scientific methods, so he found the multisource feedback credible. He decided that he was not cut out to be an administrator and chose to return to teaching and research, where he excelled.

Supervisor

Tradition drives the expectation that supervisors rate their employees, but published research consistently discredits the accuracy of these judgments due to self-serving impulses and other biases and, in some cases, lack of opportunity to observe work behaviors. Research also indicates that supervisors rate more honestly and more rigorously when their ratings are supported by other informed sources, such as with 360° feedback.

With traditional supervisor-only appraisals, the "squeaky wheel," or the loud nonperformer, often gets the "grease." Supervisors have no validating evidence for nonperformance other than their own judgment; hence, they often reward mediocrity or even nonperformance to avoid employee complaints.

Supervisor-only ratings, in comparison with other sources, such as colleagues and direct reports, tend to:

- Be inflated.
- Show less distinction among criteria.
- Show less distinction among people.

Second-Level Supervisor

The second-level supervisor, the boss's boss, usually is a very poor source of assessment information regarding employee performance because he or she has very little contact with the employee. Any information that is provided tends to be inconsistent with other respondent sources and is based more on stereotypical bias than on actual observation. Lacking an opportunity for behavioral information, second-level supervisors tend to rate on nonrelevant dimensions like height or where a person went to school. Compared to other sources, second-level supervisor ratings tend to:

- Be highly inflated.
- Be less accurate as compared with other respondents.
- Show less distinction across the various criteria.
- Show less distinction across employees.

Ironically, second-level supervisors traditionally make promotion decisions in most organizations. Without information from the employee's knowledge network, these supervisors often have to rely on politics or personal biases for evaluation and promotion decisions.

90° Feedback: Colleague Assessment

Lateral or 90° feedback comes from work associates. More than 90 percent of the published research on multisource systems examines peer evaluation, which we refer to here under the broader classification of colleague assessment. This research provides compelling evidence that colleagues, as compared to single-source (supervisory or self) judgments, provide feedback measures that are more:

- Reliable (accurate and consistent with one another).
- Valid (the highest rated people eventually receive promotions).
- Highly credible to those who receive the feedback.

Although colleagues provide high-quality input to multisource processes, they often are insufficient as the only source.

Many organizations do not have enough staff at the same level with sufficient contact to provide quality feedback, and even when enough colleagues exist, differences in experience, education, or work responsibilities can create concerns about coworkers' abilities to provide sufficiently high-quality information.

180° Feedback: Upward Review

Multiple direct reports provide 180° feedback. Ten years ago, fewer than one out of twenty-five multisource projects included upward feedback, where those reporting to the leader provided feedback. Upward feedback has been historically viewed as countercultural to traditional management thinking. (As managers said: "I give the ulcers; I don't get them.") However, organizational culture has changed significantly, and today surveys show over 90 percent of multisource assessment projects include direct reports as sources of feedback.

Direct reports may provide even slightly higher-quality information than colleagues do. As respondents, direct reports have all the positive attributes of colleagues and even higher accuracy as determined by interrater agreement, which measures the consistency of the ratings among evaluation team members. Most organizations find that both colleagues and direct reports provide accurate and credible assessments.

Leaders may worry that their direct reports will gang up on a supervisor and not provide good information. Therefore, the use of direct reports, or any other source, for input into decisions that affect employees' careers must include safeguards, such as absolute respondent anonymity, to prevent retaliation against those who do the evaluating.

Second- and Third-Level Direct Reports

Some organizations ask for feedback from "skip-level" direct reports, who are two or three levels below the supervisor. McDonnell-Douglas, for example, has found feedback from key second-level direct reports to be helpful in leadership selection. Data from second- and third-level direct reports, however, are best used as information only and should not be combined with other sources of information. These sources tend to provide little distinction in feedback across various behavioral items and do provide substantial distinction among employees.

A sample of second- and third-level direct reports, as opposed to a full census, is sufficient for gathering information.

360° Feedback

Full 360° feedback assessment assumes that feedback providers are part of the employee's circle of influence or the knowledge network, those who know the employee's work behavior best. Other sources may be team members, internal customers, or external customers.

Team Members

Team members, similar to colleagues and direct reports, typically provide excellent feedback. In a sense, team members are colleagues, and when they have sufficient contact with the employee, they provide thoughtful and accurate information.

Internal Customers

Coworkers who have sufficient work-related contact with the employee are excellent sources. As a group, their feedback tends to be similar to team members' feedback, with slightly less interrater agreement and less distinction across criteria.

External Customers

External customers may provide useful feedback that has extraordinarily high credibility with employees. External customers often prefer providing feedback to work groups or teams as opposed to individuals.

External customers are different from all other sources of feedback. They typically do not share the same culture as employees, and they tend to be slightly more positive, giving ratings from 1.5 to 2 points higher on a 10-point scale. The following suggestions pertain to using external customers:

- Keep the external customer feedback separate from other sources.
- Use external customers for information purposes until baseline and reliability issues are addressed.
- Limit the survey to five to ten items.

Growing Acceptance

Only ten years ago, few people had even heard of this new model, 360° feedback. Now, most large organizations have some experienced users, at least with informal, developmental-only processes. Moreover, the speed at which 360° feedback is being embraced by business is accelerating. The first published reference to 360° feedback in professional literature, outside of advertisements, occurred in late 1993; now the phrase is commonly used by professionals and laypeople alike. Human resources professionals, managers, and employees all see it as a commonsense approach to efficient and effective evaluation.

3

Applications for 360° Feedback

I was wrestling with decentralization because at heart I'm
a decentralizer. But . . . it became increasingly clear to
me that the real issue of effectiveness, of winning in the
marketplace, was finding ways to make the company
work horizontally.
> —Louis V. Gerstner, CEO, IBM

If you really believe in quality, when you cut through
everything, it's empowering your people.
> —Jaime Houghton, CEO, Corning

Many of the organizations that have found a wide variety of uses
for 360° feedback are debating whether these systems are best
suited for development only or for both development and performance management. Any organization embarking on the 360°
feedback process needs to consider the range of appropriate applications.

Developmental Feedback and Applications

The developmental feedback concept, championed initially by the
Center for Creative Leadership, proposes that those who are part
of an employee's circle of influence can facilitate that person's development. Developmental feedback is collected in exactly the
same way as performance feedback; the difference between the
two rests on who actually sees the resulting information.

Developmental feedback must guarantee that the information being collected is confidential to the affected employee. In other words, the employee's supervisor does *not* see the developmental feedback. The philosophy behind this concept is that the employee cannot be harmed if the feedback is not positive. This confidentiality creates an open environment:

- Employees providing feedback may be more willing to be totally honest.
- Employees receiving feedback may be more open to listening rather than being defensive.
- Employees may view the results as more credible than supervisory-only feedback, since respondents have no incentive to provide destructive ratings.
- Legal requirements for selection decisions do not have to be met, because the information does not have any impact on promotion and pay decisions.

Determining Who Sees the Results

Employees control who sees their developmental feedback. As long as the employee keeps behavior feedback confidential, such information remains developmental because the supervisor cannot take action on information that he or she does not know about.

Although many developmental-only advocates recommend sharing the behavior feedback with the supervisor, so that he or she can serve as a performance coach, this policy creates a dilemma: The supervisor cannot use the information for coaching at one time and then simply "forget" it later when making appraisal and pay decisions. Many organizations face an ethical, and potentially legal, challenge when they collect and report multisource assessment information under the auspices of developmental-only feedback and then encourage employees to share the feedback with their supervisor.

A stated policy that 360° feedback is "decoupled" or "delinked" can diminish the impact of 360° feedback on performance appraisals. However, if it becomes common for employees to share their scores with their supervisor, the process changes very quickly from development-only to development and performance. In this

Figure 3-1. 360° feedback applications for development and performance.

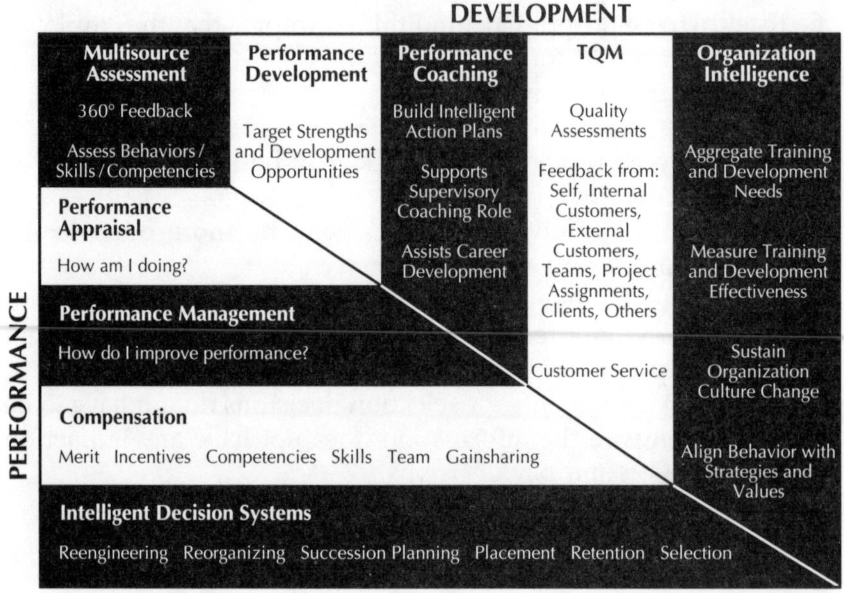
DEVELOPMENT
PERFORMANCE
Multisource Assessment
360° Feedback
Assess Behaviors / Skills / Competencies
Performance Development
Target Strengths and Development Opportunities
Performance Coaching
Build Intelligent Action Plans
Supports Supervisory Coaching Role
Assists Career Development
TQM
Quality Assessments
Feedback from: Self, Internal Customers, External Customers, Teams, Project Assignments, Clients, Others
Customer Service
Organization Intelligence
Aggregate Training and Development Needs
Measure Training and Development Effectiveness
Sustain Organization Culture Change
Align Behavior with Strategies and Values
Performance Appraisal
How am I doing?
Performance Management
How do I improve performance?
Compensation
Merit Incentives Competencies Skills Team Gainsharing
Intelligent Decision Systems
Reengineering Reorganizing Succession Planning Placement Retention Selection

case, any employee who chooses not to disclose results may be suspected of having poor behavior feedback scores.

Most organizations initiate the use of 360° feedback as a developmental tool in a manner that can help employees. Developmental applications are illustrated across the top of Figure 3-1: performance development, performance coaching, TQM, and organization intelligence. It seems hard to create an argument against improving the quality of information to employees if the result is better employee development and job performance.

Performance Development

Many 360° feedback benefits accrue to those using the process for employee performance development. Each employee can assess the information to see how he or she is serving internal customers. Note that it is up to the *employee alone* to use the information to improve performance. Since feedback from work associates motivates most people, this developmental feedback is likely to prompt constructive action on the employee's part.

Performance Coaching

Performance coaching is a useful developmental application since feedback targeted on behavioral competencies or job skills helps each associate build an intelligent action plan based on the information. The 360° feedback process creates credible behavior feedback that can be used in lieu of a performance coach to target action planning.

Total Quality Management

360° feedback creates high-quality assessments from internal and external customers, teams, project assignments, clients, and any other appropriate sources, which many organizations need in their TQM initiatives.

As a natural extension to customer service feedback, team feedback usually takes one of two approaches: feedback about the team or feedback about an individual's contribution to the team. Once users see the value of customer service feedback, they want similar feedback from internal customers directed to their team or to individuals.

Organization Intelligence

The 360° feedback process used for developmental purposes throughout the organization yields rich information for creating organization intelligence that provides a broad picture of training and development needs. Similar roll-up reports, combinations of departments, identify individual units' strengths and developmental areas.

Tracking 360° feedback scores on targeted competencies can provide measures of training and development effectiveness. For example, the behavioral impact of training can be tracked using a sequence of multisource assessments. Such information also identifies which behavior improvements, such as customer service, are sustained over time.

Developmental 360° feedback can sustain organization culture change as well. For example, Eastman Kodak created behavior feedback exclusively around creativity to recognize and reinforce individuals who most contribute to innovation in the organization. Westinghouse and Borden created a developmental behavior feedback process that focuses on safety behaviors. Culture change initiatives regarding diversity or continuous learning can be reinforced and rewarded by creating a feedback survey that recognizes and rewards those who most exemplify the behaviors associated with the new culture.

The 360° feedback process can match individual and team behaviors with organization strategies and values. When McDonnell-Douglas wanted better employee alignment with the organization's twelve values, an employee design team translated those values into specific behavior competencies. Associates at McDonnell-Douglas who demonstrate these competencies are recognized and rewarded for their support of the organization's values.

Performance Feedback and Applications

360° feedback used for performance management is the same as developmental feedback *except* that the employee's behavior feedback is shared with the supervisor, who uses this information when making a judgment of performance. Since supervisors see and use the 360° feedback results, performance management applications need to be relatively sophisticated because they potentially have substantial impact on an employee's career. Compared with development applications, performance management applications have higher requirements:

- *Job relatedness.* Do the performance measures relate to the job performed?
- *Survey development,* especially content validity. Does the survey measure what it intends to measure in understandable language?
- *Legal considerations,* including legal protection. Does the

measurement process meet or exceed the legal guidelines for selection decisions?
- *Legal and practical considerations for process training.* Have those who provide and receive feedback been trained sufficiently in the process?
- *Process and statistical safeguards.* Are predictable sources of error addressed and, where possible, eliminated using scientific principles?
- *User credibility and validity.* Do users support the process and view it as fair and valid?

These issues may not be considered important for developmental applications; even if the information is invalid, it will not directly harm an employee's career. But when 360° feedback has an impact on employees' careers, respondents may have more incentive to provide nonvalid feedback. Hence, the 360° feedback process requires more safeguards to ensure fairness to all employees.

The performance applications of 360° feedback are performance appraisal, performance management, compensation, and intelligent decision systems (see Figure 3-1).

Performance Appraisal

360° feedback used for performance appraisal helps an employee answer, "How am I doing?" The people who work with the employee regularly, which usually includes the supervisor, provide the best information to answer this question. The employee, in partnership with the supervisor, can decide how best to use this information.

Performance Management

The 360° feedback system provides excellent performance management support because it pinpoints the employee's areas of strength and areas in need of development. The behavior feedback from multiple sources is typically both comprehensive and specific.

In comparison, traditional single-source performance information typically creates bland and general feedback because single raters tend to generalize or clump large amounts of specific information together. The 360° feedback process, due to its structure, provides clear feedback on every critical skill or competency. Users can assess this information and make informed decisions about their performance plans. In addition, because the 360° feedback process is so specific, employees can track their progress on each competency.

Compensation

The application of 360° feedback to performance appraisal often leads to its use for merit pay and other compensation decisions. The information provides the necessary performance measures, which are more discriminating among performance levels than single-source measures.

The 360° feedback process can provide recognition and rewards based on competencies, skills, job behaviors, customer service scores, or team results or contributions. Some organizations also use the process to support incentive processes: bonuses, team recognition and rewards, gainsharing, and other creative reward policies.

Intelligent Decision Systems

When organizations are faced with difficult decisions, such as reengineering or reorganizing, succession planning, placement, or other selection decisions, they need solid information. The 360° feedback process has more reliability, validity, and credibility than any other performance assessment process. For example, an organization can develop intelligent decision systems for promotional decisions by tracking 360° feedback results over time. Such a tracking system can create valid selection criteria that ensure the organization places its employees in positions most suited to their competencies.

The Pros and Cons of Using 360° Feedback for Performance

The great debate seems to be whether to use 360° feedback for performance management. These issues, summarized in Figure 3-2, address the specific arguments for and against 360° feedback for performance management.

Arguments Against Performance Applications

Most of the arguments against using 360° feedback for performance-affecting decisions tend to dissolve with experience. For other arguments, solutions are available.

Feedback Will Lose Developmental Impact

The fear: When 360° feedback is used for performance management, feedback providers may avoid saying what needs to be heard, fearing the information may hurt someone's career.

Experience does not support this fear. People tend to be quite candid when they provide input to colleagues, whether the information is to be used developmentally or for performance. If an organization truly fears the loss of developmental feedback, a practical solution is to divide the survey into two parts—one developmental and one evaluative—so respondents have an opportunity to provide feedback on some items that are only developmental (and are not shared with the supervisor).

Raters Will Inflate Ratings

The fear: When feedback providers worry that the information they provide will derail someone's career, they may inflate ratings.

Field research shows that respondents are honest and relatively consistent whether the results are developmental or evaluative. Research at du Pont, Current, Inc., Fidelity Bank, Arizona State University, and Meridian Oil indicates the rating distribution does not change significantly when an organization moves from development to performance feedback. Two companies recently reported that, contrary to expectation, average scores actually went

Figure 3-2. Arguments for and against using 360° feedback for appraisal and pay.

Argument Against	Solution
Ruins development	Provide a nonperformance-affecting section
Inflates ratings	Use intelligent scoring and respondent accountability
Users manipulate the system	Use intelligent scoring and respondent accountability

Arguments for	Explanation
Already being used	Many organizations are already using the information
Market driven	Users spontaneously are developing home-grown systems
Credibility and validity	Experience and research show process validity
Employee driven	Employees are asking for the use of 360° feedback systems

down, indicating higher evaluation rigor, when they moved from developmental only to performance feedback.

Users Will Manipulate the System

The fear: Feedback providers may use invalid rating strategies to (e.g., help a friend or harm a competitor) or even collude to help themselves and injure others.

Our research shows these actions are just as likely to occur in developmental-only applications. Even in initial developmental-only projects, about one in twenty-four respondents provides obviously invalid feedback. Safeguards that hold respondents accountable for rating accuracy and validity can moderate these effects. Similarly, intelligent scoring can remove the impact of invalid respondents. (These safeguards are discussed in detail in Chapter 6.)

A MAJOR HOTEL FINDS THE NUMBER ONE MYTH ABOUT 360° FEEDBACK IS FALSE

A major hotel chain surveyed experts about 360° feedback. The executives became believers in a popular myth—that the 360° feedback process should be used only for development because its use for appraisal and pay decisions leads some respondents to manipulate the system by providing invalid ratings.

Management elected to use the process first for development and then to analyze project safeguards. To their surprise, many people still tried to manipulate the system, even when it was for development purposes only.

They concluded that the myth was false. Users did not bother to wait until the process affected performance appraisals to provide invalid ratings. The lesson learned is that a 360° feedback process, whether it is used for development or for both development and performance, should include safeguards to be sure ratings are valid and not manipulated.

Arguments for Performance Applications

It Is Gaining in Popularity

The most compelling argument for the use of 360° feedback for performance applications is that many organizations are planning to use the process for performance management.

The Market Wants It

External customers select organizations that provide the best product. One way to decide among companies offering comparable products is to look at the way in which the different organizations conduct business. Employee productivity and satisfaction, product quality, and customer service are measurable elements of 360° feedback. Many organizations that currently apply the 360° feedback process in these important areas gain insights into their company and view their 360° feedback process as a competitive advantage.

360° Feedback Is Credible and Valid

Multisource systems are more accurate, credible, and valid than single-rater systems. Academic and field research provide compelling evidence that multisource assessments are fairer than single-source systems. Does it make sense to ignore the best information available when making decisions about appraisal, pay, and promotion?

Employees Want It

Organizations that do not offer a formalized process find that employees and teams are inventing their own cumbersome, though relatively effective, multisource systems internally. Organizations that use 360° feedback information developmentally are finding that employees voluntarily share the information with supervisors. Using 360° feedback for performance management simply formalizes a process that many employees already have created informally.

The Feedback Can Be Used to Make Pay/Policy Decisions

Organizations depend on accurate and valid performance measures to make pay decisions. Failing accurate performance measures, pay distributions occur inequitably, undermining the power of pay to reinforce competencies and job performance. 360° feedback creates higher-quality performance measures that have more credibility with managers and with employees. Hence, organizations can make pay policy decisions, such as performance pay or alternative rewards, with the expectation of higher employee motivation. When employees recognize that truly high performers receive rewards, they have positive incentive to perform effectively themselves.

What Does 360° Appraisal Look Like?

Many people think 360° feedback is similar to peer evaluation with multiple judgments replacing the supervisory responsibility for evaluation. They are mistaken. The 360° appraisal model is different because the supervisor retains an important role. Applied to appraisal, it often represents a hybrid, combining the best aspects of single-source and peer evaluation.

The TEAMS Model

The team evaluation and management system (TEAMS) model offers a competency-based pay structure that considers both how the work gets done and what gets done. The model incorporates a 360° feedback component for knowledge, skills, abilities, and competencies (team evaluation) as well as a supervisory measure of results (management system):

Team Evaluation	*Management System*
How the work gets done	What gets done
Multisource or 360° feedback assessment	Single source (usually)
Supervisor plus work associates	Supervisor only (usually)
Behaviors, skills, or competencies	Results or expectations

360° feedback provides a solution for assessing behaviors associated with soft skills and employee competencies but may not be the best source for measuring results. Unlike competencies, which are displayed to a wide range of coworkers, actual results may be known only to the supervisor. Therefore, blending the 360° assessment of performance on competencies with the supervisor's judgment of results provides an effective model reflecting both how work gets done and what gets done.

The TEAMS model provides a structure for making pay policy decisions where the component weights may be a function of the trust in each part. Many organizations initiate 360° feedback with zero weighting when the evaluation component represents development only. As users begin to trust the assessment of competencies more, the multisource evaluation gains more credibility and, consequently, more weighting in the pay policy (Figure 3-3). The most commonly used weighting balances competencies and results evenly. In some cases, the 360° feedback component is weighted at 100 percent and serves to assess both competencies and results. Such models are used for special cases, for example, when many people report to one supervisor or a group works together as a self-directed team.

Two-Step Migration Path

The 360° feedback process typically works best with a two-step implementation, starting with developmental feedback and then migrating to performance management. After employees have used the process for development and like it, they naturally ask for the process to be applied to pay and performance decisions. The multisource assessment process is such a significant change in the performance model that incremental applications enhance users' understanding. Users usually readily accept multisource systems through this approach.

Moving to Performance

Initial use of 360° feedback for development is not threatening to users because it has no effect on careers. Once they have some experience with the system and are trained in the process, they can move on to performance management. Divisions of organizations like AT&T, Allied Signal, du Pont, Tenneco, the U.S. Department of Energy, Monsanto, Boeing, Intel, and Meridian Oil have migrated from developmental-only 360° feedback to both development and performance management.

Strengthening Supervisory Appraisal

Cronyism, leniency, and self-serving and other biases can be traced to the lack of accountability inherent in supervisor-only appraisals. When 360° feedback is used as a supplement to supervisory review, many of the disadvantages of traditional systems can be overcome, as the following comparison shows:

(text continues on page 58)

Figure 3-3. Weighting performance assessment components.

Team Evaluation (How) (Percentage)	Management System (What) (Percentage)	Examples
0	100	American Airlines: development-only 360° feedback to support leadership development for 16,000 employees
25	75	Fidelity Bank: initial weighting for the first year was 25 percent because 360° feedback was new; it was subsequently changed to 50:50
50	50	Westinghouse Steam Turbine Generator Division: users saw 360° feedback as credible but did not support a complete change in culture that eliminated the supervisor from the process
75	25	du Pont R&D Division: colleague review was very credible; many users had already experienced it in other R&D or academic settings
100	0	Intel: spans of supervision exceed 1:70 GMAC: used in a division that reengineered the organization into self-directed teams without supervisors

Supervisor-only Appraisal System	*360° Feedback System*
System designed solely by management or experts	Participative system development
Absolute supervisor power	Participative input from work associates to supervisors
Assumes supervisors have ability and will make accurate rating judgments	Accountability for judgments by comparison with others
Blind scoring of supervisor ratings	Consensus scored with intelligence to remove obviously invalid responses
Emphasis on supervisor's "judge" role	Coaching emphasized by supervisor
Public performance judgments	Private performance judgments
Emphasis on individual versus group performance	Emphasis on both individual and group performance
Unique evaluation criteria and rules for each person	Standardized, uniform evaluation
Faith in supervisor's fairness	Safeguards for fairness and equity
Excessive time demands for supervisors	Efficient time and resource requirements

Clearly 360° feedback both increases accuracy and supports an organization culture that defines itself as participative, empowering, team oriented, productive, and offering equal opportunity for its members to succeed and advance.

Guidelines for Performance Management

When 360° feedback is used for pay and other performance management decisions such as placement, training, and promotion, it becomes a selection tool; thus, much higher legal and administrative standards must be met because it affects careers. The guide-

Figure 3-4. Guidelines for moving 360° feedback from development to pay and appraisal.

User surveys: Users' support from satisfaction surveys should exceed 75 percent.

Anonymity: Users must have confidence that their individual ratings will be *absolutely* confidential.

Distinction: The spread of scores should clearly differentiate high, medium, and low performance.

Valid difference: The distinctions must represent truly high, medium, and low performance.

Response rates: Responses from those who provide feedback should be above 75 percent.

Administrative overhead: The time required for respondents and for process administration must be minimized and reasonable.

Invalid respondents: Respondents must be accountable for honest ratings; invalid responses—those 40 percent different from the consensus of others—should be below 5 percent.

Diversity fairness: Respondents do not systematically discriminate unfairly against protected status groups, and members of such groups should receive performance scores similar to others.

Training: Users should be trained in both providing and receiving behavior feedback.

Safeguards: Safeguards to process fairness, such as intelligent scoring which minimizes known sources of bias, are understood and supported by users.

---

lines that follow for moving 360° feedback from development to appraisal and pay are summarized in Figure 3-4.

Surveying User Satisfaction

User satisfaction surveys provide an excellent source of information for process quality. Those who use and are affected by 360° feedback systems are quite forthright about telling what things go well and what things do not. User satisfaction surveys should show 75 percent or higher satisfaction with the 360° feedback process before moving from development to appraisal. If users do not support the new process, it is unlikely the results will serve well for any purpose.

Users must make a substantial time investment in providing quality feedback to others. Failing trust and perceived value in the process, they will simply not participate.

User surveys may also be used to determine whether employees would feel comfortable using 360° feedback for appraisal and pay purposes. When participants see added value in this process and trust the results, they tend to recommend its use for performance appraisal and pay. A strong desire among employees to use the system to support appraisal and pay purposes is the most critical issue in process validation.

Guaranteeing Anonymity

An effective 360° assessment process requires anonymity for respondents, so that the feedback receivers are not able to determine who provided the information. User surveys are an effective way to determine whether users are confident that their responses are indeed anonymous. Intel, for example, selects a set of "hackers" who are charged with testing respondent security. The thinking is that if the best information systems people are unable to break through the anonymity safeguards, the process will be secure for everyone.

Without respondent anonymity, many employees will not participate in providing feedback or, if they do, their responses tend to be uniformly at the top of the scale—that is, as highly inflated as single-source assessments.

Differentiating Performance or Spread of Scores

There must be differentiation, or a spread of scores, across the performance measures if the results are to support pay decisions. These distinctions must be sufficient to make credible differential reward decisions. If all the scores are clustered at the top of range, the information is not useful, and reward decisions revert to nonperformance factors, such as politics, friendship, or popularity.

It is not uncommon to see supervisor-only ratings where 95 percent of all employees are in the top two groups. Since nearly everyone appears to be a high performer, the recognition and reward system naturally follows the performance measurement process and gives nearly equivalent rewards to all employees. Unfortunately, such a process creates an entitlement culture. Moreover, when the organization needs accurate information to make placement or promotion decisions, everyone looks alike. Failing performance measures that provide distinction among high, medium, and low performers, such systems lead to promotion and other selection decisions that only randomly reward performance.

When a large aerospace manufacturer implemented a multisource assessment process for a 3,000-employee nonexempt assembly unit without sufficient process safeguards, management found that 97 percent of the multisource performance scores clumped in the top two scale points, about the same as their historical data for single-rater assessments. The company found itself without the valuable, and valid, information it needed to make development, appraisal, or pay determinations, and within a culture that found inflated ratings the norm.

Examining Scores for Valid Difference

Distinction among participants should involve examination of both the spread of performance scores and the *validity* of the various scores. Assuming the test of distinction is made in terms of scores that clearly differentiate between high, medium, and low performers, the next step should be to examine whether people receive the performance scores they should. There are two approaches here:

1. *Examine the spread of scores for departments that include people of whom managers have knowledge.* If the score spread seems valid to leaders, the assessment process provides differentiation that is likely to be considered valid. Hence, it may migrate to appraisal and pay decisions. Managers at du Pont use this approach also to support other decisions, like talent assessment and succession planning.
2. *Compare ratings with hard performance measures.* R. J. Reynolds conducted an analysis that showed high correspondence between 360° feedback scores and field sales results

for 1,400 salespeople. When the 360° assessment data correspond to quantified outcomes like sales results, the process is sufficiently strong to support appraisal and pay determinations.

The Meaning of Response Rates

Response rates for projects should exceed 75 percent before being considered to support pay practices. (Lower response rates means many people may not receive performance feedback.) Most organizations specify a minimum of three, four, or five respondents in order to show feedback to an employee. With evaluation teams of six, a less than 75 percent response rate means about one out of seven people may not have sufficient surveys returned to receive behavior feedback reports.

A HIGH-TECH SOFTWARE FIRM HAS LOW RESPONSE RATES

Management at a high-tech software firm observed that their multisource assessment process seemed to be working and decided to move from using it for development only to pay. But when they began looking at the results, they discovered to their dismay that their process was insufficiently supported to provide feedback for many people: Due to low response rates, only about 25 percent of the population received a full set of behavior feedback reports. Hence, the multisource assessments had to be used selectively or not at all. Because of the legal issues associated with using different performance appraisal methods for different employees, the software firm elected to use the multisource assessment results solely for development.

Response rates are a good indicator of process quality because many employees will refuse to waste their time providing feedback that they do not think is adding value. Response rates are highly associated with perceptual fairness. Employees tend not to respond if they do not perceive the process as fair and accurate.

Keeping Administrative Overhead Low

Administrative overhead includes the time required for respondents to complete assessment surveys as well as process administration. Experience shows that multisource processes that require substantial respondent time quickly fail because respondents cannot or refuse to take the time necessary to provide thoughtful feedback. Hence, respondent time needs to be kept to a minimum.

Administrative time is probably the biggest obstacle to 360° feedback. Few organizations have a department of employees dedicated to administering and collecting surveys, scoring them, and reporting the information. Hence, total administrative time should be minimized or the process will not be supported, even if it provides good information. For example, one McDonnell-Douglas facility decided to eliminate the multisource process because the administrative overhead was too burdensome, even though over 88 percent of users supported its continued use.

Dealing With Invalid Respondents

The move from development to pay assessment in 360° systems may motivate some people to try to "game the system" to their favor by providing invalid responses. A response is invalid when the person makes a rating that tends to the scale extremes—at the top or at the bottom—although the probability that any single person is uniformly outstanding or terrible is nearly zero. Invalid responses occur when one person's assessment is more than 40 percent different from other responses over 40 percent of the time. They occur as well when people collude. Because invalid respondents can create substantial distortion in 360° feedback projects, they need to be identified, classified, and held accountable. Once a policy decision is made of what constitutes an invalid respondent, the percentage of invalid respondents should be less than 5 percent.

A respondent validity policy may be analogous to public policy for a car pool lane. If car pool lanes are not enforced, the lane will quickly become congested with single-driver cars. Similarly, a 360° feedback system that provides no accountability for invalid respondents will encourage respondent policies that are inappropriate, such as friendship, collusion, or competition bias. The information that is provided will be so distorted that it is useless, even for development purposes. (Respondent validity issues are addressed in Chapter 6.)

Adding to Diversity Fairness

The multiple respondents should be diversity fair—that is, the information they provide should show that they did not systematically discriminate on the basis of age, gender, color, or any other protected classification. Problems in this area can be discerned by asking two questions when analyzing respondent feedback:

1. Toward which individuals is a respondent consistently inconsistent (either significantly higher or lower) with others on the evaluation team?
2. Are these systematic inconsistencies directed toward a member or members of protected-status groups?

Similarly, the performance scores as a whole should be audited to ensure that a substantial or unexplainable difference does not exist among demographic categories, such as ethnicity, gender, or age. Explainable differences are those based on education or experience, for example.

The issue of diversity fairness should be addressed prior to moving to appraisal. Otherwise the 360° feedback process is likely to discriminate against protected groups. Fortunately, recent research for over 23,000 employees who received 360° feedback across three different organizations provides encouraging indicators that results were positive to age and neutral to gender and ethnicity (see Chapter 9).

Providing Training

Because of legal requirements for performance appraisals, users of 360° feedback—those who provide and those who receive it—need to be trained. Independent of legal requirements, employees need training in any new appraisal system. 360° feedback may call for more training than traditional systems because the new model is so different, though most employees easily understand the modest changes associated with redesigning a supervisory appraisal form. Nevertheless, 360° feedback systems offer an opportunity for employees to participate in a wide variety of process elements—

instrument development, evaluation team selection, and providing feedback for others—and must understand how these work.

Developing Safeguards

Safeguards to process fairness are critical to the process and can be tested in user surveys. Policy safeguards seek to ensure the content validity of the evaluation criteria and the validity of the policy for selecting evaluation team members. If safeguards are unavailable to address every concern users have about the process and data integrity, 360° feedback should not be used for appraisal and pay decisions. Multisource processes without safeguards predictably result in a loss of data integrity and a loss of support for users, who rightfully do not trust the process or the results.

Designing for Fairness

As organizations increasingly use 360° feedback to support both development and performance management, they must remember to ask those who use the process if it adds value, is fair, and is appropriate for appraisal and pay decisions. The user safeguards can eliminate the predictable effects of potentially invalid respondent strategies, which is especially critical when using 360° feedback for performance management. When everyone knows the process is fair, people stop trying to manipulate the system, and employees and management receive the high-quality performance information they expect and deserve.

Part II
Implementing 360° Feedback

4

Designing a 360°
Feedback Project

Fail to honor people,
They fail to honor you;
But of a good leader, who talks little,
When the work is done, his aim fulfilled,
They will all say, "We did this ourselves."

—Lao-tzu

The greatest magnifying glasses in the world are a person's own eyes when they look upon his or her own person.

—Alexander Pope

Leadership and learning are indispensable to one another.

—John F. Kennedy

The 360° feedback process represents a dramatic change in performance assessment for many employees and organizations. As it supports and encourages employee participation, it also adds to employee responsibilities. The design, implementation, and evaluation processes are described in a ten-step process flow model (Figure 4-1):

Phase I: Process Design
   1. Select the application.
   2. Develop a competency-based survey.

Figure 4-1.   Model for designing a 360° feedback process.

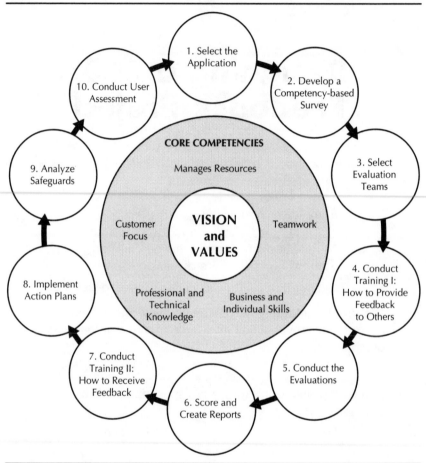

Phase II: Process Implementation
   3. Select evaluation teams.
   4. Conduct training I: How to provide feedback to others.
   5. Conduct the evaluations.
   6. Score and report the results.
   7. Conduct training II: How to receive feedback.
   8. Create action plans.

Phase III: Process Evaluation
   9. Analyze safeguards.
  10. Conduct user assessment.

Each action is explained in this and the following two chapters. This chapter outlines how an organization creates the 360° feedback process (Phase I). Chapter 5 covers Phase II, the important details of implementing the 360° feedback process. Chapter 6 highlights Phase III, the evaluation stage, in which an organization determines the success the 360° feedback process and identifies ways to fine-tune it for the next feedback cycle.

Before an organization begins to implement a 360° feedback process, its leaders or key change agents need to commit to the process, select a design team, and create a communication plan to inform employees about the new process. Among the most critical issues is attaining leadership support.

Leadership Support

Like any other major change, senior leadership support accelerates the adoption of the 360° feedback process. The leadership team may be the first or an early group to receive behavior feedback. Many organizations pilot a 360° feedback project with a group of fifty to one hundred participants who are not part of the top management group. After the pilot test, the communications, training, and process actions can be refined to fit the needs of employees and management better.

Although support by the senior leadership team is preferable in implementing 360° feedback, anyone who acts as a change agent at any level of the organization may take the initiative to create this process. Organizations considering the adoption of 360° feedback often find that individuals from many different departments and functions have spontaneously initiated a variety of informal, and sometimes formal, multisource assessment processes.

The Design Team

When a 360° feedback project is initiated, by top leadership, a manager, human resources, or an employee, a user design team smoothes the way. A design team composed of six to fifteen employees from various organization levels and functions shares the responsibility for designing, implementing, and assessing the 360° feedback process, and it ensures employee involvement and assists with communication.

Determining Organizational Readiness

The design team assesses organizational readiness for 360° feedback by determining whether the organization's environment and culture support such a process. The self-scoring readiness assessment form in Figure 4-2 offers a way to make this determination. Scores of over 100 predict smooth and successful adoption of 360° feedback.

Projects are most successful when top management supports the process. Especially important is managers' willingness to serve as role models and receive feedback from those in their circle of influence. Too often managers initiate multisource assessment systems that apply to others but not to themselves. Obviously, such actions limit employees' commitment to the new assessment model.

Organizations that have already communicated the need to recognize and reward both individual and team performance and the need to support performance or competency-based management find adoption relatively smooth because employees already understand the process philosophy. Similarly, adoption is quicker when employees know that performance includes both how they go about their job and the results.

Dissatisfaction with the existing performance feedback and appraisal process helps to justify the change to a new model. For example, when employees feel they are not receiving helpful performance feedback, a multisource process offers an obvious solution. Similarly, employees who want their individual performance and teamwork recognized and rewarded are likely to embrace 360° feedback.

Organizations that use customer feedback regularly to support quality initiatives often find that 360° feedback systems are a logical next step. And where some managers already use informal feedback methods, formalizing the process makes sense. Organizations that use multirater processes, such as selection panels and committees for selection and placement decisions, often find em-

Figure 4-2. Self-scoring readiness assessment for 360° feedback.

Don't Know	Strongly Disagree		Disagree			Agree			Strongly Agree	
N	1	2	3	4	5	6	7	8	9	10

Please rate the degree to which you agree with each statement on a 10-point scale, where 10 is highest.

Score (1-10)
1. Top management supports decisions at the lowest possible level. ____
2. Business results blend individual and team performance. ____
3. Policy supports performance-based management. ____
4. Management wishes to align vision, values, and job behaviors. ____
5. Managers are willing to serve as role models for receiving feedback. ____
6. How work gets done, as well as what gets done, is important. ____
7. Units or teams set shared objectives. ____
8. Developmental feedback is encouraged. ____
9. Employees are not satisfied with the current performance feedback. ____
10. Customer feedback and TQM measures are embraced. ____
11. Some managers already solicit feedback from others. ____
12. Managers talk to others before making selection decisions. ____

Scoring
Over 100: Aligned with 360° feedback concepts: 360° feedback will be embraced.
Over 80: Some support: 360° feedback will need some support.
Under 80: Uphill battle: 360° feedback needs substantial communications and support.

ployees view 360° feedback as a natural extension to current practice. Usually the less change that is required to implement a 360° feedback process, the more quickly and easily the process will be adopted.

Ironically, some of the fastest process adoptions occur in organizations with scores below 50 on the readiness assessment. The reason is that when discontent is very high, employees may view any change as positive. For example, some organizations have initiated 360° feedback to overcome such problems as cronyism and bias or in response to widespread dissatisfaction with the current performance appraisal process.

After assessing readiness, the design team is ready to develop a vision statement identifying desired outcomes for the 360° feedback project.

Identifying the Objectives

A number of objectives may be identified for the new process:

- To align individual and team behavior with corporate vision and values.
- To focus on competency-based rewards.
- To provide fair and accurate performance measures.
- To support a commitment to continuous learning.
- To reinforce other organizational initiatives (e.g., customer service, teamwork, quality, empowerment, performance-based rewards, or reengineering). The 360° feedback process then serves as a communication tool that helps employees understand how their behavior connects to the organization's objectives.

An effective two-step method for developing process objectives is to (1) ask design team members for their thoughts on process objectives, which can be collectively refined as a draft set, and then (2) send the draft list to key organizational members for their thoughts. Once sufficient people have provided their upgrades to the process objectives, they should be come an important part of what is communicated to employees.

Many organizations identify the objective of increasing employees' satisfaction with the organization's performance measurement and appraisal system. A short pretest, such as that shown in Figure 4-3, provides an indication of how satisfied users are with the current, usually single-source, performance feedback and measurement system. This baseline information is a valuable measure of process effectiveness and can be used to compare to postimplementation satisfaction with the new system.

Figure 4-3. Evaluation for the current appraisal process.

Don't Know	Strongly Disagree	Disagree			Agree			Strongly Agree	
N	1	2	3	4	5	6	7	8	9	10

The current performance feedback and measurement process provides me with information that:

1. Is useful for development.................. N 1 2 3 4 5 6 7 8 9 10
2. Is useful for appraisal..... N 1 2 3 4 5 6 7 8 9 10
3. Motivates me................ N 1 2 3 4 5 6 7 8 9 10
4. Is valuable for me.......... N 1 2 3 4 5 6 7 8 9 10
5. Is fair to me.................... N 1 2 3 4 5 6 7 8 9 10
6. Is fair to others.............. N 1 2 3 4 5 6 7 8 9 10
7. Is a complete assessment..................... N 1 2 3 4 5 6 7 8 9 10
8. Is an accurate assessment N 1 2 3 4 5 6 7 8 9 10
9. Provides safeguards for fairness .... N 1 2 3 4 5 6 7 8 9 10
10. Overall, I am satisfied with current process ...... N 1 2 3 4 5 6 7 8 9 10

11. Comments:

About you: (optional)
Time in job: ____ under 1 year ____ 1 to 3 years ____ 3 to 5 years
____ 5 to 10 years ____ 10+
Time in firm: ____ under 1 year ____1 to 5 years ____ 5 to 10 years
____ 10 to 20 years ____ 20+
Gender: ____ Female ____ Male
Age: ____ under 30 ____31–40 ____ 42–50 ____ 51–60 ____ 61+
Race: ____ Asian or Pacific Islander ____ Black ____ Caucasian
____ Latino ____ American Indian or Alaskan native
____ Other
Education: ____ high school ____ 2 yrs. college ____ 4 yrs. college
____ graduate degree
Manager ____ Nonmanager ____
Number of direct reports: ____

Creating a Promotion Plan

Effective communication is paramount to the success of the 360° feedback system. Once the objectives are clearly stated, they must be communicated to all employees. Anticipating concerns and communicating how the organization will address challenges smoothes the adoption of the 360° feedback process. Figure 4-4 shows an example of an announcement.

The promotion plan communicates all of the implementation steps while also promoting the benefits to each employee, answering, "What's in it for me?" Organizations may create a special set of newsletters or an insert to its regular communications, such as the company newsletter, a president's message, or e-mail. An example of a newsletter is shown in Figure 4-5 and an example of a time line in Figure 4-6.

Planned communications need to address the following typical user concerns:

- Why is the organization adopting this process?
- What is the purpose of the process?
- What are the tie-ins with other initiatives, such as quality or employee involvement?
- Who will participate as feedback receivers and as feedback providers?
- How were the competencies developed?
- Who was involved in designing this new system?
- How are evaluation teams selected?
- How have issues such as fairness, accuracy, and time requirements been addressed?
- What are the major policy guidelines? For example, how will the information be used?

Selecting an Application

With leadership commitment and a design team in place, the organization may be tempted to dash through some important de-

(text continues on page 79)

Figure 4-4. Sample project announcement letter.

To: All Employees

Alpha Labs has been examining a new employee development and assessment called 360° feedback. This new assessment method allows employees to receive feedback from those in their circle of influence, such as self, supervisor, colleagues, direct reports, internal customers, and others.

A design team made up of Alpha Labs employees at all levels and from many functions has created the architecture for this new process. I can tell you from firsthand experience that this process feels a lot different from the old one when you receive feedback from those with whom you work. It looks very promising, and we expect the process to enhance our current appraisal system by improving:

- Employee perception of fairness in performance evaluation.
- Employee understanding of our core competencies or success factors.
- The quality of performance information received for employees and for supervisors.
- Information available to develop and assess teamwork.

We expect the 360° feedback to replace the nonintegrated assessment tools we currently have with one evaluation instrument, which is more reflective of our current work styles.

Your team has been selected as a pilot group to determine if this process can effectively support a field workforce with a diversified skills set. We will be listening to your feelings about the process, so please examine it by participating and give your candid assessment.

To begin this pilot, a focus group of field Alpha Labs employees recently met to develop a competency-based instrument incorporating our values. You will use the competencies to provide feedback to others.

Subject to your supervisor's approval, you will be selecting those you work with most closely to provide you feedback. The 360° feedback process includes many safeguards to maximize fairness to everyone.

There will be a two training sessions supporting the 360° feedback projects. In the first session, you will be provided orientation and training about the 360° assessment, the competencies to be rated, the selection of raters, the time line for results, and how the information will be processed. Attached is information about the 360° feedback process for your review prior to the session. The session will be held from 8:00 A.M. to 10:00 A.M. on September 21 in the employee meeting room.

I am excited that we have been selected to work on this project and I appreciate your support.

Figure 4-5. Sample newsletter.

During the remainder of the year, you will be hearing about a new performance development process that your organization is piloting. It is called 360° Feedback. A pilot has been approved, in support with senior management, to study this unique concept. Approximately 100 employees throughout the organization will be participating in this pilot.

Employees have indicated that the current performance development and appraisal process does not work well. It does not provide them feedback information that they can use to improve performance. The 360° Feedback process provides a more accurate performance evaluation through the use of multiple evaluators. By soliciting evaluation input beyond the immediate supervisor, higher-quality performance information is gathered.

An implementation committee has been established to help implement the process. The implementation team members are [names listed]. If you have any questions or comments on the new 360° Feedback process, please call one of the team members to discuss.

A tentative implementation schedule has been developed:

April Survey of behavioral competencies distributed to pilot participants for comments. Implementation team to revise draft and redistribute by the end of January.

May "How to Give Feedback" training will be provided for all pilot participant employees. This is the introduction to the process. The benefits of the 360° process will be discussed. Pilot participants will learn the important steps necessary to receive individual performance feedback.

Evaluation team selection forms to operator.
Surveys distributed to all evaluators.
Surveys completed by employees and returned to the operator for scoring.
Process surveys and generate reports.

June "How to Receive Feedback" will be provided for all pilot employees. This session will describe the feedback reports so you can interpret the feedback information. Using the information to develop individual action plans will be covered. This is the most important training session on 360° Feedback! A postimplementation evaluation survey will be distributed to find out from employees whether pilot participants recommend continuing to use the process.

July Postevaluation survey evaluation results distributed.

A pilot group of approximately 100 employees will participate in the first phase. These participants will be selecting an evaluation team of coworkers and clients to assess their performance based on the behavioral competencies. For the pilot, evaluators may be selected from anywhere in the organization.

Figure 4-6. Sample project time line.

Action	When
Develop draft instrument	Weeks 1–2
Review policy decisions	Weeks 1–2
Develop instrument and instructions	Week 3
Finalize instrument and instructions	Week 4
Conduct "How to Provide Feedback"	Week 4
Select evaluation teams/distribute surveys	Week 4
Complete evaluations	Weeks 5–7
Process data and generate feedback reports	Weeks 7–8
Conduct "How to Receive Feedback"	Week 9
Conduct and survey of pilot participants	Week 9
Analyze results of pilot and prepare recommendations for next step	Week 10

sign steps to get right to the point where employees provide feedback. They should not because the design phase is key to the project's success. Decisions at this stage have an enormous impact on project quality and, especially, users' assessment of fairness and value. Therefore, the design team needs to turn its attention to selecting the application and developing a 360° feedback, competency-based survey.

Many organizations initiate 360° feedback projects not for performance management and pay applications but with the strategic intent of leadership or career development, identifying training needs, customer service, team assessment, team building, or other actions designed for individual, team, or organizational improvement. Borden, for example, put together a project tied to training and development for the purpose of supporting safety, and Eastman Kodak's project sought to recognize, develop, and reward innovation and creativity. When performance management is a goal, applications include performance planning, appraisal, compensation, recognition and rewards, placement, talent assessment, training effectiveness, and succession planning. Most performance applications support both development and performance management.

The design team should consider the benefits and drawbacks to using 360° feedback for development and performance applications, and then decide which application is appropriate for the organization. Our best advice is to keep the application simple. After testing the process in a pilot project, other features can be added.

A pilot project, like a shakedown cruise, can identify key issues that can create severe problems in process roll-out if they are left unresolved. A pilot may include fifty to one hundred participants and represent key organizational groups. To keep the pilot simple, two or three intact groups, such as departments, participate. Design team members too need to participate in the pilot project so they can see firsthand how their proposed process works.

Developing a Competency-Based Survey Instrument for Feedback

Competencies are underlying characteristics that identify high and low performers and are relevant to both the organization and its employees. Organization competencies, sometimes called *core competencies,* are those qualities that distinguish an organization from its competitors and establish value in the minds of its customers. These competencies relate to the firm's products or services and are also the bundle of knowledge, skills, and abilities employees bring to their work. A core competency for customer service could be written as follows:

> Partners with internal and external customers to assess needs and establish and prioritize goals for action.

A competency-based rewards system recognizes what people accomplish at work rather than rewards them for acquiring additional knowledge or skills. When core competencies are communicated to employees, they understand the behaviors that distinguish good from poor performance. Articulated core competencies also allow the organization to create a competitive advantage by differentiating itself in the marketplace and helping it to achieve its goals and objectives.

Survey development, also called *instrument development,* is often the most difficult and lengthiest task of the 360° feedback project because of the importance in achieving content validity and user support. One excellent way to select the competencies for the survey is to organize a focus group—a cross-functional group of employees from various organizational levels who will use the 360° feedback system. Members of this team should:

- Represent all organizational levels (management, individual contributors, and, if applicable, union members), key organizational functions, and key roles.
- Include at least one well-known skeptic (these people are often not hard to find).
- Possess strong communications and language skills.
- Be high performers.

The focus group's job is to answer the question: "What are the critical competencies our organization will need in the future to sustain our competitive advantage in the marketplace?" By articulating the factors that lead to and sustain individual, team, and organization effectiveness, the focus group helps to define the individual behaviors that support broad organization goals and objectives. The agenda shown in Figure 4-7 is one way for the focus group to go about its work.

As the group identifies competencies to support the organization vision and values, it develops statements associated with each value that become questions on the survey. These statements should be clearly written, in the active voice, and brief. (Long statements are tedious to read and unnecessarily increase response time.) Competencies usually need some definition, which may be provided with illustrative behaviors. For example, the competency "presents ideas clearly" may be defined as:

- Modifies message to be understood by receiver.
- Keeps messages direct and simple.
- Uses straightforward language.

The core competencies or success factors may be further refined, with examples of high performance on a specific competency in various functions of the organization, and reflect as well the professional and technical expertise required in a particular job

Figure 4-7.   Agenda for a survey development focus group.

- Purpose, objectives, importance of 360° Feedback
- Share vision, values, principles, and strategy of organization
- Discuss 360° feedback principles and process
- Highlight "Leadership 20/20"; *What critical competencies are necessary to compete in the year 2000 and beyond?*
- Summarize behavioral criteria

- ◆ Activity I—Develop
  List critical behavioral criteria: *What are the behaviors critical to effectively achieving the organization's mission in the year 2000?*
  Goal: Maximum number of behavioral criteria
- ◆ Activity II—Expand
  Enrich behavioral criteria based on additional information
- ◆ Activity III—Combine similar constructs
  Sort behaviors into clusters or groups
- ◆ Activity IV—Combine lists to one flip chart
  Aggregate behavioral criteria for each team on a flip chart
- ◆ Activity V—Refine
  Reconsider groupings and items within groups
- ◆ Activity VI—Behavioral descriptors
  Develop behavioral descriptions for the behaviors

function. Some organizations develop competency models specific to individual job functions or families. Others develop a single survey for all levels of the organization. When the organization wants alignment with a specific vision and values, a single survey best communicates the behavior norms of the new culture.

The competency-based assessment survey shown in Figure 4-8 is called Leadership 20/20. It represents a composite of over sixty 360° feedback projects across a wide variety of public and private organizations. Each of these sixty organizations used its own assessment instrument, but their content of the specific competencies included many of the items used in the Leadership 20/20 survey. Figure 4-9 shows the competencies and the key values in a wheel shape, which can be extended to show how second-level competencies can be used to further first-level competencies define.

text continues on page 86

Figure 4-8. Leadership 20/20 assessment survey.

Feedback Receiver: _____

What is your relationship to the individual you are rating (please fill in the appropriate circle).
- Self .... "I am evaluating myself."
- Manager .... "I am evaluating the employee as his/her manager."
- Colleague .... "I am evaluating a colleague within my department."
- Direct Report .... "I am evaluating my manager."
- Internal Customer ..... "I am evaluating a colleague/team member outside my department."
- Other.... "I am evaluating a person who does not fit into the above groups."

You have been identified by the individual being rated in this evaluation as one of a number of individuals who can provide valuable input to the employee on his/her performance. Your individual responses will remain anonymous (unless you are the employee's supervisor); only composite information will be provided to the employee.

How well does this person perform this competency? Please use the following scale for your evaluation:

(9–10) An Exceptional Skill   This individual consistently exceeds behavior and skills expectations in this area.

(7–8) A Strength   The individual meets most and exceeds some of the behavior and skills expectations in this area.

(5–6) Appropriate Skill Level   The individual meets a majority of the behavior and skills expectations in this area for this job. There is generally a positive perspective toward responsibilities.

(3–4) Not a Strength   The individual meets some behavior and skills expectations in this area but sometimes falls short.

(1–2) Least Skilled   The individual consistently fails to reach behavior and skills expectations in this area.

(N) "Not Applicable" or "Not Observed"

CUSTOMER SERVICE
Treats customers like business
   partners ....N 1 2 3 4 5 6 7 8 9 10
Identifies, understands, and responds to
   appropriate needs of customers....................N 1 2 3 4 5 6 7 8 9 10
Presents ideas simply and clearly....................N 1 2 3 4 5 6 7 8 9 10

(continues)

Figure 4-8. (continued)

Listens actively to internal and external
   customers ....N 1 2 3 4 5 6 7 8 9 10
Solicits and provides constructive and
   honest feedback ....N 1 2 3 4 5 6 7 8 9 10
Keeps others informed ....N 1 2 3 4 5 6 7 8 9 10
Balances requests with business
   requirements ....N 1 2 3 4 5 6 7 8 9 10

TEAMWORK

Supports team goals ....N 1 2 3 4 5 6 7 8 9 10
Puts interest of team ahead of self ......N 1 2 3 4 5 6 7 8 9 10
Builds consensus and shares relevant
   information ....N 1 2 3 4 5 6 7 8 9 10
Recognizes and respects the contributions
   and needs of each individual ....N 1 2 3 4 5 6 7 8 9 10
Actively seeks involvement/uses input
   from people with different
   perspectives ....N 1 2 3 4 5 6 7 8 9 10
Builds and maintains productive working
   relationships ....N 1 2 3 4 5 6 7 8 9 10
Treats others, such as diversity group
   members, fairly ....N 1 2 3 4 5 6 7 8 9 10

BUSINESS AND INDIVIDUAL SKILLS

Demonstrates broad business knowledge
   and skills ....N 1 2 3 4 5 6 7 8 9 10
Acts to add value to the business ....N 1 2 3 4 5 6 7 8 9 10
Recognizes problems and identifies
   underlying causes ....N 1 2 3 4 5 6 7 8 9 10
Makes timely decisions ....N 1 2 3 4 5 6 7 8 9 10
Coaches and develops others ....N 1 2 3 4 5 6 7 8 9 10
Is trustworthy, open, and honest ....N 1 2 3 4 5 6 7 8 9 10
Visualizes the present and future and
   develops strategies to get there ....N 1 2 3 4 5 6 7 8 9 10

PROFESSIONAL AND TECHNICAL KNOWLEDGE

Demonstrates professional/technical
   expertise ....N 1 2 3 4 5 6 7 8 9 10
Improves existing processes and/or
   introduces new methods ....N 1 2 3 4 5 6 7 8 9 10

Actively increases personal skills,
knowledge, and technology base ....N 1 2 3 4 5 6 7 8 9 10
Contributes personal expertise to others............N 1 2 3 4 5 6 7 8 9 10
Organizes work ....N 1 2 3 4 5 6 7 8 9 10
Motivates others to achieve results
through example and
encouragement ....N 1 2 3 4 5 6 7 8 9 10
Acts dependably to get things done
right the first time ....N 1 2 3 4 5 6 7 8 9 10

MANAGES RESOURCES
Takes initiative to make things happen..............N 1 2 3 4 5 6 7 8 9 10
Makes informed, calculated risks ....N 1 2 3 4 5 6 7 8 9 10
Makes well-reasoned, timely decisions ....N 1 2 3 4 5 6 7 8 9 10
Follows through to deliver results ....N 1 2 3 4 5 6 7 8 9 10
Uses resources efficiently..................................N 1 2 3 4 5 6 7 8 9 10
Communicates a clear direction ....N 1 2 3 4 5 6 7 8 9 10
Anticipates and prepares for change ....N 1 2 3 4 5 6 7 8 9 10

Comments: _____

Most organizations initiate a 360° feedback project with a single survey, but some develop additional competency sets for special groups or purposes. For example, an individual competency like "Communicates" can be refined with second-level competencies such as oral, written, listening, public presentation, nonverbal, and other specific behaviors.

Allied Signal and Tenneco use a set of core competencies for all employees. Those who lead others—supervisors and managers—receive feedback on an additional set of six to eight functional competencies associated with leadership. Eastman Kodak created a secondary set of competencies built around creativity and innovation. A person who receives 360° feedback scores that are lower than desired on creativity can self-initiate a second survey using twelve key behaviors associated with creativity. The secondary competency sets allow employees to receive very specific feedback in various areas. Customizing the survey by combining competency sets allows the organization to meet the assessment needs of special roles or functions while still using a survey with the organization's common core competencies.

Figure 4-9. Leadership 20/20 competency model.

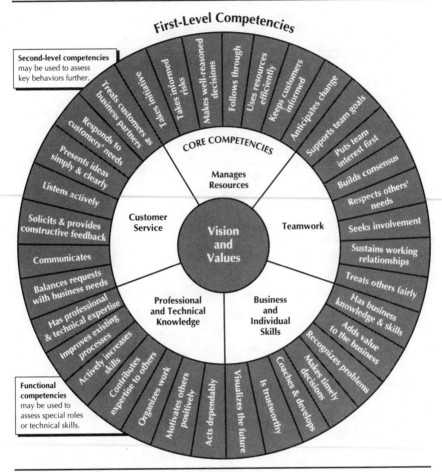

Functional competency sets may be developed for any specific function or role. Technical skills sets are often used as functional competencies for design engineers, information systems scientists, and research scientists. Similarly, field salespeople may find value in using a set of competencies relevant specifically to field sales.

Some organizations create extensive illustrations of key behaviors. CONOCO, Westinghouse, and the Equitable Insurance Company have used illustrations describing extremely high and low levels of performance for each competency. Although research does not support the need to create illustrations of this sort to get reliable assessment information, illustrations nevertheless provide excellent training for respondents.

Regardless of which approach is adopted, surveys should:

- Match competencies to the organization's vision and values.
- Focus on critical behaviors and skills that differentiate the organization in the marketplace.
- Use the organization's common language.
- Use simple language that all organization members understand.
- Group similar content together, such as competencies associated with teamwork.
- Keep the competency set simple and short.

The development team's draft survey does not have to be perfect initially; the pilot study will point out areas where changes are needed. To maximize validity, the instrument development process should:

- Survey a cross-functional set of employees.
- Allow for review of the survey by the design team and executive, legal, human resources, and functional users.
- Allow for a pretest of the survey to assess readability, completeness, and clarity.
- Include a pilot of the survey with a new group of employees or outside reviewers.
- Plan on continuous refinement to the survey based on user experience.

The Appendix contains samples of competency assessments for 360° feedback.

Types of Surveys or Instruments

Many organizations purchase a standardized survey from an assessment vendor in order to skip survey development so they can

Figure 4-10. Standardized and customized instruments: a comparison.

Standardized Instruments	Customized Instruments
Useful for development-only feedback	Useful for developmental feedback, performance appraisal, or both
Generic behaviors or style	Organization- or job-specific competencies
External validation	Validation is usually internal
External norms available (external norms may be invalid)	Internal norms only (internal norms will have credibility)
Many instruments are long	Instruments of any length
Relatively expensive ($50 to $600 for each use; usually must pay a royalty)	Inexpensive (no instrument cost for each use)
May not align with organization's vision and values or core competencies	Targeted to fit organization's needs and align with vision and values
May be too general to be credible	Specific and credible skills and competencies
Language may be academic, generic, and not relevant to job	Language understandable, credible, and relevant to job
No internal buy-in and possibly weak content validity	High buy-in and content validity because the employees (users) developed the constructs

immediately begin gathering multisource feedback. These widely available standard surveys use general constructs that apply to leadership roles typical to most organizations. Figure 4-10 compares standardized and customized surveys.

Several important considerations must be evaluated prior to using a standardized survey:

- How will the results be used? For development only? For performance? Both?
- For whom was the survey designed? Self? Supervisor? Peers? Others?
- For whom was the survey validated?
- How many questions are in the survey?

- How long does it take to complete?
- How high is the percentage of nonresponses likely to be?
- Is the survey useful for this organization?
- What are the costs for first use and for repeat use?

Standardized surveys lack features that may be necessary when the instrument will be used to make decisions with an impact on the employee's career, including training, merit, pay, promotion, and retention:

- Content validity within the user organization.
- Job relatedness, in terms of critical competencies, for effective performance.
- Process validity, including safeguards to ensure respondent anonymity and data integrity.

Nevertheless, some organizations have made the mistake of taking standardized surveys valid for developmental feedback only and using them for performance management. A valid survey used in an invalid process is likely to produce invalid results. Standardized surveys are *not* valid for performance management because they are not tied to specific performance requirements for the organization. A customized survey is appropriate for performance management because it reflects the organization's vision and values and clearly communicates the organization's unique core competencies.

Experimenting with a standardized survey often helps organizations choose between customized and standardized surveys. With experience, the design team can make more informed decisions regarding the need for customizing a survey.

Other Survey Design Issues

Several other survey design issues are relevant to the design process.

Scale Variations

Various 360° feedback applications such as job analysis may use a scale such as importance. An importance rating examines the relative criticality of each competency. Such projects often analyze the most critical competencies or success factors for each job or job family. The resulting prioritization of competencies for each job provides useful information for selection decisions. Concerns with specific job requirements, such as resulting from the Americans with Disabilities Act, may be addressed by multiple employees' assessing how critical various competencies are for particular jobs.

Some 360° feedback processes use a combination of scales, such as importance, criticality, difficulty, or frequency, alone or in combination with performance. For example, the 16,000 employees who participated in the 360° feedback process at American Airlines received measures for each construct regarding both importance and performance. For the competency "Takes initiative," respondents were asked:

- How important is it to the performance of your job that this person takes initiative?
- What is this person's performance on "Takes initiative"?

Importance scales help those providing feedback emphasize what they see as most important, and importance and performance measures together help employees target developmental areas. A low importance rating paired with a low performance rating may indicate a low priority for developmental attention. Conversely, a high importance score paired with low performance should alert the employee to turn attention to that area as soon as possible.

Those who are designing a 360° feedback project need to consider these questions when selecting scales:

- Will additional scales add value? How much?
- Will people know how to interpret feedback on importance?
- Is the additional complexity valuable?

Scale Anchors

Scale anchors help respondents understand the various levels of performance represented on a rating scale. Descriptors "anchor" the scale by tying a specific narrative description of a scale position. Most scales have anchors at least at the top and bottom. Following is a typical rating scale:

(9–10)	An exceptional skill	This individual consistently exceeds behavior and skills expectations in this area.
(7–8)	A strength	This individual meets most and exceeds some of the behavior and skills expectations in this area.
(5–6)	Appropriate skill level	This individual meets a majority of the behavior and skills expectations in this area for this job. There is generally a positive perspective toward responsibilities.
(3–4)	Not a strength	This individual meets some behavior and skills expectations in this area.
(1–2)	Least skilled	This individual consistently fails to reach behavior and skills expectations in this area.
(N)	"Not applicable" or "not observed"	

Although these anchors are shown for a 10-point scale, a 5-point scale can be used with the same descriptors, with only 1 scale point for each descriptor. For example, the top point, 5, would represent "an exceptional skill," a 4 would be "a strength," and so on. Respondents should always have a nonresponse option, such as "I do not know" or "no opportunity to observe." Lacking a nonresponse option, respondents may provide inaccurate feedback if they lack sufficient information yet feel compelled to provide a response.

The exact wording used to describe the various scale points has little impact on the precision of the resulting measures. However, the use of too few scale anchors, such as only two to describe the high and low end of the scale, usually elicits complaints for not having a middle-point option. Other commonly used scale anchors may include the following:

Poor; fair; good; very good; excellent
Never; almost never; sometimes; usually; always
Very low; low; average; high; extraordinary
Not at all; not often; often; very often; nearly always
Ineffective; somewhat ineffective; solid contributor; very effective; extraordinary
Needs improvement; development area; meets expectations; a strength; exceptional
Not evident; less evident; evident; sometimes evident; highly evident
Strongly disagree; disagree; neutral; agree; strongly agree
Not critical; somewhat critical; critical; very critical; extremely critical
Not important; low importance; important; high importance; critical

The reliability of 360° feedback derives from the fact that multiple people respond independently to the scale. Respondents who share the same basic culture typically are very consistent in how they interpret scale anchors. A change in the scale anchors usually results in a very similar assessment results.

Consistent response to scale anchors does not always hold true for all cultures and for those whose primary language is not English. For example, compared to the response pattern by Americans, a service firm found the response pattern different in Tokyo for those for whom English was their second language or who responded to a Japanese translated instrument. More research is need in cultural variations in assessments.

Some organizations create behaviorally anchored rating scales for each competency and provide examples for each point on the scale (Figure 4-11). Behavioral anchors take a long time to develop, though, they usually are specific to a job, and they substantially increase respondent and administrative time. Moreover, they add little, if anything, to the quality of the resulting performance measures and 360° feedback systems in general. Multisource assessments gain their accuracy from averaging the perceptions from multiple independent respondents, not from the precision of narrative scale descriptors.

Some organizations have tried unbalanced scale anchors, with the midpoint description below the middle—for example:

Poor	*Good*	*Very good*	*Excellent*	*Walks on water*
1	2	3	4	5

The intent of unbalanced scales is to move respondents to the lower part of the scale in order to decrease anticipated rating inflation. Unbalanced scales, however, are neither necessary nor valid. Research shows that some respondents do not recognize the unbalanced scale and use the rating scale as if the middle were average. And respondents who misread or did not read the scale are combined with those who interpret the scale literally. Hence, unbalanced scales are likely to create substantial respondent errors.

The best design advice is to keep surveys and survey elements simple and understandable.

Scale Width

If the 360° feedback process is intended to communicate information to employees about their behaviors and to motivate behavior change, the use of a wider scale adds value. Narrow scales are fine for large sample surveys, but 360° feedback systems use a sample size of four to seven respondents, often with little variance in response. A narrow scale, such as a 5-point scale, results in flat profiles that provide little motivational impact to the employee. A 5-point scale, as shown in Figure 4-12, typically results in mean responses of 3.8, with a very narrow range of scores, from about 3.4 to 4.2. When all scores look the same, it is hard for those who receive feedback to feel motivated to change a behavior that is less than half a scale point different from a strength. Also, with a narrow scale, measurement error may exceed the range of scores aver-

(text continues on page 96)

Figure 4-11. Behaviorally anchored scale for leadership. *Source:* Adapted from Southern California Edison.

Performer:

GUIDELINES	10	20	E 30	40	Value Baseline 50	60	Preferred 70	80	90	Ideal 100	Evaluation
Place an "X" in the square that best represents your perception of each element. DO NOT SCORE.											
ACCOUNTABILITY Demonstrates ownership accountability for his or her own actions (not excuses), and the actions of his/her AOR.	Blames outside sources for failures; dismisses or discounts any indication that his or her actions contributed to the final outcome.		Takes responsibility but seeks to reprimand someone.		Accepts responsibility for making *some* choices that influenced team's ability to overcome obstacles.		Shares his or her mistakes with members of group, accepts responsibility for his or her actions and actions of team members.			Takes full accountability for actions of his or her team; encourages and defines clear parameters for individual decision making, and creates a learning environment.	
RISK TAKING Demonstrates support for others who take risks even if they fail.	Reprimands employee when impact(s) of risks taken are significant.		Coaches me at review time on the impacts of the risks I have taken.		Gives me timely feedback on the actions I've taken and supports my decisions.		Encourages my taking risks where I feel deviations from policy are appropriate to our objectives.			Reinforces all members of group who take intelligent risks with positive recognition; also celebrates learning experiences.	

PARTICIPATIVE MANAGEMENT Allows employees to participate in organization planning and decision making.	Informs us of direction and decisions made; offers little flexibility in altering those decisions.	Involves me only at the task level.	Attempts to reach consensus with group on decisions that affect our team's outcomes.	Involves members of group on most of the organization planning and decisions.	Strategic direction and decisions are made by consensus of the group, with guidance from our supervisor.
DELEGATION AND DEVELOPMENT Delegates challenging assignments to employees according to both individual and organization.	No rationale to the assignments our team is given. Equity of distribution is unfair.	Assignments are appropriate to my level of competence.	Provides me with challenging work assignments and clear direction.	Fairly delegates challenging assignments to most members of the group.	Inspires everyone in the group to seek out new and challenging work assignments and to delegate for themselves.
COMMUNICATION Effectively communicates and garners commitment to department strategic direction.	Information seems filtered, and on a need-to-know basis.	Communicate changes in direction when prompted by senior management.	Informs me on how I contribute to the department's strategic goals, and updates me on changes or new focuses.	Actively seeks ideas/suggestions from group or department's focus and provides feedback to senior management.	Consistently provides our group with unfiltered, timely information and feedback that keeps us focused and committed to meeting our objectives.

Figure 4-12. Behavior profile on a 5-point scale.

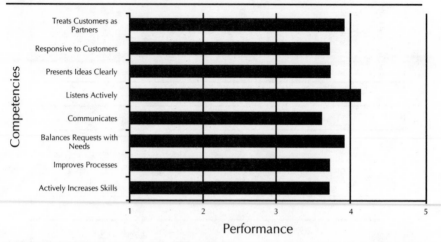

ages. Hence, the results could be due to chance or measurement error, rather than the true intent of the respondents.

A wider scale, such as a 10-point scale, results in far richer profiles that show a greater difference among behavior criteria. The profile resulting from the wider scale in Figure 4-13 has far more shape, with greater difference between high and low scores, than the relatively flat profile associated with a 5-point scale. The richer profile motivates behavior change because the differences between strengths and developmental areas are more visually obvious.

The typical response pattern to various scales is shown in Figure 4-14. Respondents prefer wider scales because they are able to show shades of difference, especially at the high end of the scale. Those receiving the behavior feedback prefer them as well because the information they receive clearly points out strengths and developmental areas.

Any scale can be used to provide 360° feedback. However, if an important goal is motivating behavior change, a wider scale may be the best choice. Remember the insightful words of William James: "Differences that do not make a distinction do not make a difference."

Figure 4-13. Behavior profile on a 10-point scale.

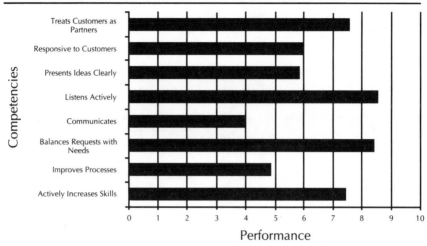

Survey Length

Consider those who provide feedback when making survey decisions, especially the length of the instrument. The key question is: "How long will respondents devote to providing high-quality feedback to others?" Remember that each person typically provides feedback to five to twelve individuals for each cycle of the 360° feedback process, and the longer the survey is, the more time is required to complete each survey.

Research suggests that after only about 15 minutes, survey respondents become fatigued or frustrated. People are able to respond to about three survey questions per minute. Hence, a reasonable 360° feedback survey probably should use between twenty and thirty-five items. If the survey takes twice as long to complete, research shows, more than twice as many people fail to respond at all to the survey. In a long survey, often more than twice as many nonresponses occur on the second half of the survey compared with the first half. In addition, respondents are likely to provide significantly less distinction among items on the second portion. When respondents get tired, they seem either to stop responding or to make all their ratings about the same.

Figure 4-14. Typical responses to different scales.

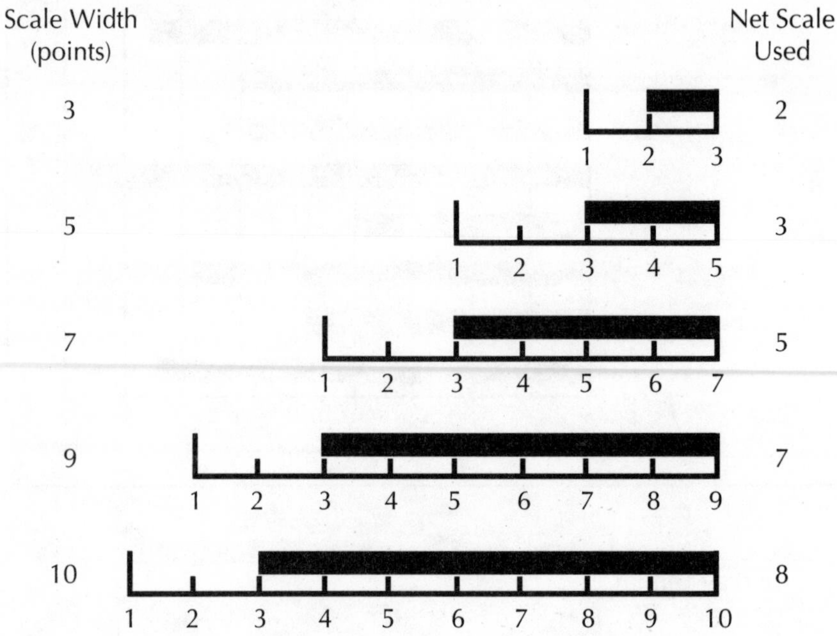

Scale Width (points)		Net Scale Used
3		2
5		3
7		5
9		7
10		8

Survey Timing

When the 360° feedback will occur is usually driven by business issues. Conducting the process on a focal point, one six-week period, is the most common method. A focal point minimizes administrative overhead because the process occurs all at one time. However, a focal point schedule may mean that some respondents will have a particularly heavy burden if they must participate in a number of assessments.

When 360° feedback is attached to pay, some organizations use an anniversary date as a prompt for the assessment. An easier plan to administrate, developed by OXY USA, schedules feedback four times a year. Anyone with an anniversary date in the second quarter gets feedback during the first quarter. The quarterly schedule is manageable and provides fresh feedback in time for annual performance reviews.

The other timing question is how often to use the process.

Many design teams initially think they will use 360° feedback three or four times a year. After they experience the process, they are likely to become more conservative. Most organizations use 360° feedback once a year; some use it twice a year—once for development only and once for performance. Research indicates behavior feedback changes insignificantly when feedback occurs more often than twice a year. Users quickly discover how little behaviors change in short periods and are unlikely to be willing to provide feedback on a nearly continuous basis.

The availability of automated, online 360° assessment systems has prompted a sensible new practice, with one mandatory assessment conducted each year and employees' or managers' initiating additional feedback surveys as needed. Timing feedback to users' requests makes the process flexible and accommodates a wide variety of development and assessment needs.

A Model for System Design

The SUCCESS model provides a checklist for a 360° feedback system design. The process design elements should maximize each of the SUCCESS factors to achieve the project objectives, create strong measures, and obtain strong user satisfaction measures:

The SUCCESS Model

Simple	Easy to understand and to use
Understandable	Users understand what, why, and how to take action
Competency driven	Built on the organization's critical competencies
Communicates clearly	Communicates important behaviors and competencies
Equitable	Fair to all participants
Shares the vision	Aligns behaviors with vision and key values
Sustains enthusiasm	Motivates and sustains behavior change

Reflections on the Initial Stage

Effective 360° feedback projects do not spontaneously happen. A successful process requires thoughtful consideration of the design elements and extensive employee involvement. Targeting the specific application and developing the core competencies are logical first steps in this process.

5

Implementing 360° Feedback

If winning does not matter, why does anyone bother to keep score?
—Adolph Rupp, basketball coach, University of Kentucky

The ablest man I ever met is the man you think you are.
—Franklin D. Roosevelt

Once an organization has selected the application for 360° feedback and designed a competency-based survey, it can begin putting the feedback process in motion. Implementation, however, is more than just handing out surveys and pencils. It encompasses many elements, from selecting evaluation teams to implementing action plans.

Select Evaluation Teams

Users are naturally concerned about what will be evaluated and who will do the evaluation. Usually the process design team develops a policy on who will provide feedback for each person. The guidelines typically emphasize the selection of six or more coworkers: supervisor, colleagues, direct reports, internal customers, or others in a position to provide thoughtful feedback.

Some organizations recommend additional respondents, often for political reasons or because they want more people to be involved. For example, supervisors may want a minimum of their manager, four colleagues, and four direct reports. Since a minimum of three responses needs to be received to report feedback from any perspective, supervisors usually select four or more. The response minimums are a safeguard to protect the anonymity of those who provide feedback.

Evaluation teams larger than six are unnecessary from a measurement perspective. Additional respondents typically provide no new information and simply repeat what others report. Larger evaluation teams also add significantly to the time needed to support the process. Nevertheless, evaluation teams representing different perspectives, such as colleagues and direct reports, can result in variations in the feedback. Hence, selecting team members with different perspectives often adds important information.

The following questions may help determine members of evaluation teams:

- What policy and selection safeguards will create the best perceived fairness?
- What policy will yield the most trustworthy results for users?
- How many others do most people interact with sufficiently to provide quality feedback?
- Who is in the best position to know who can provide credible feedback?
- How will special circumstances be addressed?

Special circumstances include people who interact with only a few others, have contact with only direct reports, not colleagues, or who serve on staffs where they interact for short periods, with many different internal customers.

Most commonly, each employee is allowed to select his or her evaluation team, with possible revision and sign-off by the immediate supervisor. Houlihan's Restaurants added a feature to respondent selection that has become popular in many 360° feedback projects: Supervisors may add to, but not subtract from, the employee-selected evaluation team. Employees find this fair because the supervisor supports rather than overrules the employee.

Conduct Training I: How to Provide Feedback to Others

The training guidelines for users are simple: Invest in training, or forget about 360° feedback. Many multisource assessment implementers skip training, thinking that the process is so straightforward that training is unnecessary. Then they wonder why employees do not support the new process.

Users usually anticipate the opportunity to provide and receive feedback with some anxiety. Training on providing and receiving feedback that highlights the benefits of this process can set their minds at ease. Failure to train users in the process is like asking a pilot to fly without instruction. The likelihood of failure is great.

The initial training, "How to Provide Feedback to Others," introduces employees to the 360° feedback process, outlines the steps, and instructs respondents on how to complete behavior feedback surveys. The initial training addresses the following common questions that users ask:

- What is 360° feedback?
- Why is the organization adopting this new model?
- What's in it for me?
- How can I be sure that the ratings I make of others will remain anonymous?
- Who will see the results, and how will the results be used?
- How should I provide feedback?
- What are my roles and responsibilities?
- What is the process time line?
- How can I avoid making errors when I am a respondent?
- What safeguards are there to ensure the process is fair?

During training, employees should be asked if they have used group consensus or multisource assessment in another setting. Many participants have; someone may have used a similar process to judge a contest, select leaders in professional and community groups, or choose projects or vendors. Building on similar multisource experiences provides confidence that the process will work to everyone's benefit. At least twenty minutes of this approximately 2-hour training session should be devoted to user questions and answers.

Conduct the Evaluations

The evaluations should be conducted fairly, quickly, and simply. People want a convenient process that yields a fair outcome. Users do not support labor-intensive 360° feedback processes because no one wants to do the required tedious work. The 360° feedback system must be simple, or the process itself will create errors.

Survey response time should be short—less than 15 minutes. Since most respondents provide feedback for five to twelve others, respondent fatigue represents a critical variable. Respondents should limit the length of time spent completing surveys at any one time to about 1 hour. Providing thoughtful feedback requires effort, so respondents should be encouraged to allow uninterrupted time for this task.

Mode of Data Collection

Gathering feedback information can be accomplished in a variety of ways: paper survey forms, optical scan forms (where respondents fill in bubbles with pencils), or automated data capture, such as e-mail, computer disk, or online modes. The advantages and disadvantages of various data collection methods are shown in Figure 5-1. The trend in 360° feedback systems of collecting the information electronically reduces administrative overhead, improves respondent confidence in anonymity, and is perceived by respondents as faster. In tests where people have responded on paper and electronically, nineteen out of twenty preferred electronic input.

Most organizations opt for a mixed-mode collection process. A less formal pilot process often uses simple paper surveys. Faster and more secure methods, such as disk or network based, are used as the feedback process becomes more formal. Formalized scoring methods require high levels of data security and administrative complexity that are difficult or impossible to guarantee with paper surveys. In 1995, about 10 percent of users who use a PC-based system still responded on paper, due either to computer anxiety or lack of convenient access to a computer. Hence, most 360° feedback systems incorporate multiple modes of feedback collection.

Before selecting the mode of feedback, consider the advantages of online input as compared with paper surveys. Online process modes:

- Create higher confidence in respondent anonymity.
- Increase in the number of narrative comments four to six times for each participant.
- Are perceived by users as faster and more convenient.
- Can provide on-screen help and coaching to avoid response errors.
- Allow nonrespondents to be identified and reminded to complete their assigned surveys.
- Allow translation of competencies into other languages for users who do not speak English.
- Reduce administrative overhead substantially.
- Reduce data collection errors.

User surveys show that respondents perceive that they can complete the evaluative portion of online surveys more quickly than with paper surveys. Also, it turns out that respondents provide far more and far better narrative comments online in comparison to paper surveys. Automation offers greater flexibility to match specific needs within the organization more closely and improves the quality of feedback.

Intel decided a paper-based assessment process was not only too costly in terms of staff time but also antithetical to its goal of a paperless office. Its online survey input reduced supervisory response time to a fraction of that required by traditional paper-based evaluation processes.

American Airlines has used the 360° feedback process since 1987. More than 16,000 employees have participated in its Committing to Leadership process, which includes 360° feedback from colleagues and direct reports. Participants average forty-seven pieces of paper for each assessment process, including instructions, envelopes, and surveys. They also receive nine to twenty-one pages of

Figure 5-1. Pros and cons of various methods of collecting feedback.

Mode	Disadvantages	Advantages
Paper	Requires substantial administrative overhead Low perceived anonymity Key entry expensive and subject to errors Few narrative comments	Easy to create Little or no training required
Scan-forms (paper)	Requires substantial administrative overhead Low perceived anonymity Expensive scan forms require five to eight weeks to print Almost no narrative comments Few safeguards supported	Little or no training required Data input errors are low
Telephone (users respond on a telephone using the keypad)	Does not save time (users fill out paper forms and use phone for input) Respondents may not take input seriously, creating spurious feedback Low perceived anonymity Subject to response errors No narrative comments	Easy to train Excellent access (everyone has access to a phone) Especially good for external customer input
Fax (users respond on paper and fax in ratings)	Low perceived anonymity Subject to errors No narrative comments	Easy to train Excellent access Expecially good for external customer input
E-mail (users respond on their e-mail system)	Low perceived anonymity Subject to errors No narrative comments Requires E-mail access	Easy to train Especially good for narrative comments

Mode	Disadvantages	Advantages
Disk (users respond on a PC diskette encrypted for security)	Requires specialized software Must have access to a PC	Easy to train users (10 minutes) Faster response than paper High perceived anonymity May provide on-screen help, criteria definitions, and scale description Very convenient for users Increases narrative comments four to six times over paper Allows automated surveys at any time
LAN or **WAN** (Local or wide area network)	Requires access to a networked PC Higher initial cost than disk	Easy to train users (10 minutes) Faster responses than paper High perceived anonymity May provide on-screen help, criteria definitions and scale description High convenience Increases narrative comments four to six times over paper Allows online surveys at any time

feedback reports. Automated assessment for this project makes sense because it saves about 1 million pages of paper: 752,000 pages for survey administration and 240,000 pages for reports.

The following questions are helpful in determining which method to use:

- Do participants know how to use a PC? If not, is training available?

- Does everyone have access to a PC in their work area?
- Are narrative comments important?
- How important are respondent speed and anonymity?
- Are sufficient resources available to administer a paper process?

Safeguards for Data Collection

Data collection should include safeguards so that the source of individual feedback is not identifiable in any manner to the employee. Using an inappropriate mode of collecting feedback, such as a telephone survey that does not ensure respondent anonymity, predictably creates data errors and undermines process integrity. If respondents do not feel the information they provide is absolutely secure, they may either refuse to participate or provide uniformly inflated evaluations. Failure to ensure respondent anonymity has a negative impact at both ends of the process: those who provide the feedback do not trust the process, and those who receive feedback do not trust what they read.

Score and Report the Results

Organizations must score and report results carefully. Improperly scored or reported data that have been effectively collected can create serious information errors. Informal and formal methods for scoring provide useful information.

Informal Scoring

Scoring multisource feedback for a small group can be done quickly with a hand calculator, a spreadsheet or database management program, or a survey system. Such methods are simple, fast, and cheap. However, simple systems work only for developmental feedback because they are likely to report data with substantial errors due to the small samples associated with 360° feedback systems. Informal scoring simply aggregates the multiple responses for each employee and creates a summary report.

AN ELECTRONICS MANUFACTURER'S INFORMAL FEEDBACK SYSTEM FAILS MISERABLY

An electronics manufacturer used a process in which employee surveys and comments were returned to the supervisor, who created a summary report for each direct report. This system cost the organization nothing explicitly but created a huge burden on supervisors; moreover, returning the surveys directly to the supervisor created the perception of loss of respondent anonymity. Hence, the scores were skewed toward the top of the scale, and comments were generally neutral and provided little value to employees.

The organization tried to help preserve anonymity by asking supervisors to edit the narrative comments. Its good intent, though, totally backfired. Employees did not like receiving comments that were changed. They complained that the editing could manipulate what was said and that they would not know what the actual comment was. Additionally, some of the supervisors sanitized the comments by making many changes, others none. Finally, the process of typing comments and editing them was very tedious and led to spelling and content errors.

The results of this system devastated the integrity and acceptance of the multisource process. The company found that less than 10 percent of the users were satisfied with the informal multisource assessment system.

Formal Scoring

Formal scoring goes beyond simple spreadsheets and survey systems and uses the best available scientific methods to score surveys with small samples. Formal scoring systems correct predictable sources of bias, such as invalid respondents, and identify data errors like respondent collusion. An organization that fails to use a formal scoring method for 360° feedback applied to making performance management and pay decisions will regret this choice. Data errors will multiply and users will have no confidence in their behavior feedback.

Figure 5-2. Impact of an outlier rating of "1" when all others were "8."

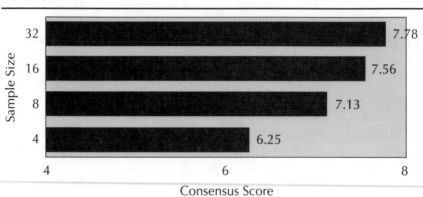

Scoring Safeguards

Scoring safeguards maximize the fairness of the 360° feedback information. Unlike traditional single-source systems, multisource assessments can use computer analysis to identify and eliminate invalid respondents. Invalid respondents may be identified using scientific principles that indicate judgments that differ from all others beyond reasonable chance.

One highly discrepant respondent, or *outlier,* can substantially skew the average score because there are often so few respondents. (An outlier gets its name from the concept that the unusual response falls a significant distance outside the range of the other scores.) Without discounting the outlier, the resulting score would not represent the collective intent of the multiple respondents. It would reflect a skewed score, which might be due to error intentionally created by one respondent.

The substantial impact on small sample scores from one outlier is illustrated in Figure 5-2. In the figure, all respondents except one made ratings of 8; one respondent, the outlier, rated 1. When the sample size is large—thirty-two or even sixteen—there are plenty of other scores to dampen the effects of one high discrepant response. The score mean for thirty-two respondents is 7.78, which is very close to 8. However, the one discrepant respondent skews the score mean to 6.25 when there are only three other scores to moderate the impact of the outlier. This is why traditional survey research requires large sample sizes in order to make reliable decisions.

360° feedback presents a very different scenario. Unless the highly discrepant respondent is eliminated, employees will get results that contain substantial error. Unfortunately, this error most severely affects the highest and lowest performers—exactly the people for whom accurate measurement is most needed for both motivation and for administrative purposes like raises and promotions.

A MANUFACTURER CONFRONTS THE OUTLIER IMPACT

The president of a large manufacturing firm became concerned about the multisource process when a senior vice president received very low scores. This executive had been on a fast track for several years and had a uniformly excellent reputation. Nearly everyone thought she was the leading contender for the presidency. The president asked for a review of the informal multisource assessment process because the result was so aberrant from what seemed to be the collective wisdom.

Project analysis showed a number of flaws that led to her low score. Data collection had occurred over the telephone using the touch-tone keypad, without safeguards such as respondent anonymity. Consequently, most employees' scores were at the extreme top of the scale. The scale inflation was made worse by the use of a 5-point scale, because nearly everyone used the top two scale points.

Analysis of the vice president's situation indicated that she had received nearly uniformly high responses from three respondents but all low marks from another one. Although she had selected a team of nine respondents, fewer than half had responded. The response pattern of only "1"s on the rating scale was clearly invalid, since no one could make a persuasive argument that this corporate star was unsatisfactory on every competency. Yet this obviously invalid evaluation had a substantial impact on her scores. And since nearly all other employees had received high scores too, the single outlier pushed the vice president's scores down into the bottom quarter of all performers.

These results were clearly not the intent of the multiple raters, who collectively rated this person as a high performer. However, one person, possibly feeling a competitive bias, nuked her. Such response patterns obviously are invalid and should be removed from multi-source scores. The process was modified to use trimmed mean scoring and other safeguards to maximize the probability that the collective wisdom of those who provided feedback was represented in the next assessment.

Trimmed mean scoring, which discounts the extreme high and low responses, and thus removes nearly all outliers, serves as a useful safeguard. Trimming the highest and lowest rating provides three major advantages: a more stable mean, freedom from respondent guilt from injuring someone, and better respondent anonymity. Eliminating the extreme high and low ratings provides a more stable mean for the small sample than a simple mean or average. This also is called *Olympic scoring* because it is used to promote fairness and reduce the potential effects of nationalistic bias in the Olympic games.

Respondents usually want to be honest and provide both positive and negative information, but they do not want to be responsible for singularly damaging someone else's career. Trimmed mean scoring relieves this concern because if a respondent's judgment is off base, it will be eliminated. Only when a number of people feel the same way will others receive critical feedback.

Possibly most important, trimmed mean scoring offers additional respondent anonymity. Since everyone's score could have been the one eliminated, no one individual can be singled out for providing the criticism. User surveys have shown that over nine out of ten respondents prefer trimmed mean scoring.

A consistent concern about trimmed mean scoring is that valuable information will be lost. This concern can be accommodated by retaining the narrative comments that accompany trimmed responses.

Internal or External Scoring?

Organizations must decide whether to collect and score data internally or externally; both methods have benefits and disadvantages.

Preserving respondent anonymity often drives the decision

for external scoring and reporting, because the raw data are not kept within the organization. Since someone outside the company takes on this administrative burden, only nonemployees have access to the actual ratings. This not only improves anonymity but relieves supervisors or an internal process administrator of additional responsibilities. The drawback to external scoring is the substantial and recurring expense.

Fortunately, recent technology innovations have improved this process. Outsourcing part or all of a 360° feedback process may make sense when security is critical, such as with executive assessments, or when on-site administrative resources are limited. Automated outsourcing also can substitute PC diskettes for paper in an organization that lacks a network. Automation reduces administrative costs substantially because there is no need to handle outbound and inbound paper surveys.

An outsourced process works as follows:

1. The automated software for selecting evaluation teams and creating and selecting surveys is set up within the organization and then administrated remotely.
2. The remote administrator uses a modem to make the same administrative actions as would an administrator on-site.
3. Participants on site select evaluation teams, supervisors approve the evaluation teams, and participants provide feedback by using personal identification numbers.
4. The remote administrator notifies nonrespondents and regularly moves the encrypted rating files off-site for secure scoring and reporting.
5. The 360° feedback reports are returned to each participant. Management reports are returned to the human resources department.

Many organizations are finding that respondent anonymity can be maintained with internal scoring as well. When safeguards are used and explained, participants understand that their responses will be kept completely anonymous. When internal scoring is supported with user training, it is not unusual for more than 90 percent of users to report satisfaction with the preservation of respondent anonymity.

At the British Columbia Institute of Technology, employees made a concerted effort to break into an internal scoring program as a check of program security. When the experts could not break into the program, they declared it secure. Nevertheless, many organizations still outsource scoring and reporting when sufficient anonymity, either real or perceived, cannot be ensured internally.

The following questions may be helpful in determining whether to score the surveys within the organization or outside it:

- What are the costs of internal scoring and outsourcing? (Outsourcing generally costs considerably more than internal scoring, and the costs are incurred every year.)
- Are sufficient staff available to administer the process internally?
- Will internal staff have sufficient knowledge and interest to administer the process?

Make or Buy the Software?

Many organizations initially use nonsophisticated scoring to avoid technology costs. A spreadsheet or survey program to score and create basic reports can be constructed in a few days. As users become more sophisticated and aware of data errors, however, they need more formalized data collection and scoring methods, which mean an investment in software. Amortized over several years, the investment in available software is relatively small—less than $20 a person—and the software can be used repeatedly at no additional cost. The following questions are helpful in assessing whether to create a formalized and automated 360° feedback system internally or to purchase software:

- What is the cost of creating an automated 360° feedback system?
- Can human resources get authorization to create and sustain a 360° feedback system?
- What is the cost of process and technology testing?
- Can we create sufficient process and technology safeguards internally?
- What is the cost of maintaining and upgrading our own software?

- What is the cost of process validation?
- What is the cost of process training development?
- What is the probability and cost of failure for an internal process?
- What is the legal risk associated with creating a behavior feedback process that turns out to be invalid because we lacked sufficient expertise in this area.

Reporting Results

Reports should be simple and statistically sound, and use the best available methods for presenting the information. Feedback reports also should be easy for users to understand. Minor alterations in reporting can affect users' motivation to accept and use the feedback and affect their perception of the process and its credibility.

A NORTHEASTERN HEALTH CARE SYSTEM REPORTS THE SCORE RANGE— AND WISHES IT HAD NOT

An experience at a northeastern health care system illustrates how a minor scoring issue may create a major, and possibly disastrous, process issue. Because one of the design team members was trained in traditional large sample survey systems, the project design decided to report the score range. When Bob received his behavior feedback report, he was stunned:

Competency	Score	Range
Communicates with others	7.8	2–9

Although he received a good score, 7.8, thanks largely to the trimmed mean, he focused instead on the range. He was furious that someone had rated him a 2! What was his most likely next action? It has been called "headhunting." Most of Bob's efforts focused on ferreting out the singular person who was very unhappy with him.

A better solution than a range is to show a measure of respondent variation, such as the standard deviation or an index of respondent variation, that people can easily understand.

A SOUTHWESTERN HEALTH CARE SYSTEM FINDS ITS TIMING OF PROVIDING THE REPORTS IS OFF

Modest issues associated with behavior feedback reports can jeopardize an entire 360° feedback project. A southwestern health care system piloted a multisource project and decided to send the behavior feedback reports to both the employee and supervisors at the same time. What had seemed to be a good idea caused substantial flack. Some supervisors called in their direct reports to discuss the evaluations before the direct reports had a chance to digest the information. Some direct reports went to their supervisors enraged that the supervisor's rating was lower than others and wanted to know why.

The timing for feedback works best if the subjects—the employees who were assessed—first receive feedback, preferably supported by training. Shortly after, supervisors receive the reports with the instruction to hold reports for a few days before conducting coaching sessions. A little time allows both employees and supervisors to think about the results and prepare for a thoughtful discussion.

The report formats illustrated in Figures 5-3 to 5-7 have tested very well in user assessments. A sample of comments on the person who is profiled is illustrated in Figure 5-8. Narrative comments may be available in some projects without the evaluative, rating scale reports.

Reports may use symbols to represent information. The report cover page in Figure 5-3 explains the symbols. For example, the trimmed mean performance score is represented by a P. Various respondent perspectives are represented by: s = self; S = supervisor, C = colleague; D = direct report; I = internal customer; and O = other.

An R represents the number of people who responded on each item. An A indicates the degree of agreement or spread of scores for each item—that is, how consistently the evaluators are with all others. An A score below .5 indicates low agreement among the respondents; therefore the person who receives feedback should recognize the measure as less reliable that other scores, which show high agreement. The A score is calculated from the standard deviation of ratings *before* the extreme high and low ratings are trimmed.

Figure 5-3. Cover page for a 360° feedback report.

ABC Corp. Developmental Assessment 1		
May 3, 19x4		
Evaluator Type		*Number of Evaluators*
Self .... s:		1
Supervisor .... S:		1
Colleague .... C:		7
Direct Report .... D:		5
Group .... G:		14

Key: P = Performance
    R = Respondents, Number of
    A = Agreement, Degree of
        Where A = 1.00 Perfect Agreement
            A > .75 Very High Agreement
            A > .50 High Agreement
            A < .50 Low Agreement

The criteria ranking report in Figure 5-4 arrays the competencies from highest to lowest scores. A quick look shows which competencies are strongest and which most need development. Users are often coached to look at what groupings of competencies fall at the top and bottom of this report. For example, if technical skills are clustered near the top and interpersonal skills toward the bottom, an action plan addressing interpersonal skills may provide the most value.

In the profile report in Figure 5-5, the competency scores are shown in the order they were presented on the instrument. The profile is also useful for comparing feedback from various time periods since the results stay in the same order.

The factors report in Figure 5-6 summarizes competency sets or values. For example, the teamwork factor encompasses the seven individual competencies shown on the competency wheel (Figure 4-9), such as "supports team goals," and "puts the team interests first."

The perspectives report in Figure 5-7 breaks out the feedback by type of respondent. The gaps between self scores and the super-

Figure 5-4. Criteria ranking report.

Supports team goals

P: 7.82

Puts interest of team ahead of self

P: 7.44

Builds consensus and shares relevant information

P: 6.91

Recognizes and respects the contributions and needs of each individual

P: 6.82

Actively seeks involvement/uses input from people with different perspectives

P: 6.78

Builds and maintains productive working relationships

P: 6.40

Treats others, such as diversity group members, fairly

P: 6.40

Demonstrates broad business knowledge and skills

P: 6.36

Acts to add value to the business

P: 6.27

1   2   3   4   5   6   7   8   9   10

Average of performance scores

Note: P = performance score.

visor, self, and others may provide valuable insight. Often the perspectives report shows variations in response by different respondent types. Usually only the person who receives the feedback can decide which is more important—for example, feedback from colleagues or direct reports. Which information is most critical is often determined by the circumstances associated with a job. A person who works primarily with colleagues may view their

Figure 5-5. Profile report.

		R	A
Supports Team Goals	S ▓▓▓ . s . . . . . . P: 7.44	11	0.81
Puts Team Interest First	s . . S . . . . . . P: 6.91	13	0.48
Builds Consensus	.S s . . . . P: 6.40	12	0.73
Respects Others' Needs	S ▓▓ . . . s . . . . . P: 6.82	13	0.52
Seeks Involvement	S ▓▓ s▓ . . . . P: 6.27	13	0.76
Sustains Working Relationships	S ▓ . . . . s . . . . . P: 6.40	12	0.79
Treats Others Fairly	S ▓▓ . s . . . . P: 5.64	13	0.52
Has Business Knowledge and Skills	S ▓▓▓ s . . . . P: 6.78	11	0.61
Adds Value to the Business	S ▓ . s . . . . P: 5.45	13	0.54
Communicates	S ▓▓ . . . . s . . . . . P: 6.27	13	0.45
Recognizes Problems	S ▓▓ . . . s . . . . . . P: 5.82	13	0.47
Makes Timely Decisions	S ▓ . . . . s . . . . . P: 6.36	13	0.47
Coaches and Develops	S ▓ . . . . s . . . . . P: 6.27	13	0.56
Is Trustworthy	S ▓▓▓ s . . . . . . P: 7.82	13	0.57
Visualizes the Future	S ▓▓ s▓ . . . . P: 6.18	13	0.52
COMPOSITE SCORE	S ▓▓ . . s . . . . P: 6.46		

```
|----|----|----|----|----|----|----|----|----|
1    2    3    4    5    6    7    8    9    10
```

Note: S = supervisor evaluation; s = self-evaluation; P = performance score; R = number of respondents; A = degree of agreement (>.75, very high; >.50, high; <.50, low).

Figure 5-6. Factors report.

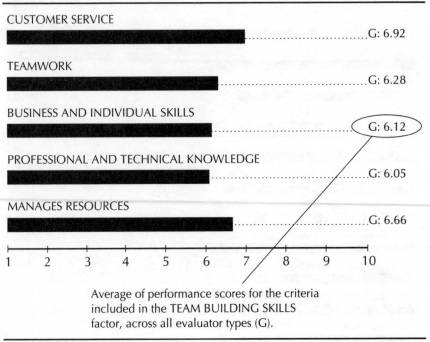

CUSTOMER SERVICE
....G: 6.92

TEAMWORK
....G: 6.28

BUSINESS AND INDIVIDUAL SKILLS
....G: 6.12

PROFESSIONAL AND TECHNICAL KNOWLEDGE
....G: 6.05

MANAGES RESOURCES
....G: 6.66

1   2   3   4   5   6   7   8   9   10

Average of performance scores for the criteria
included in the TEAM BUILDING SKILLS
factor, across all evaluator types (G).

input as most critical, while a person whose primary work contact is with direct reports may see their feedback as most important. Most users recognize that 360° feedback does not change the importance of the supervisor's feedback. The boss is still the boss.

Narrative comments may be structured so they are competency specific. All the comments in Figure 5-8 about customer orientation, for example, are grouped. General comments follow the competency-specific comments. Most comments are anonymous, but sometimes people want others to know who made a specific comment.

Narrative comments are not as anonymous as rating scale input. A very specific comment may indicate special information that gives away the feedback provider. However, most people quickly learn to make comments that are constructive and specific yet anonymous.

Figure 5-7. Perspectives report.

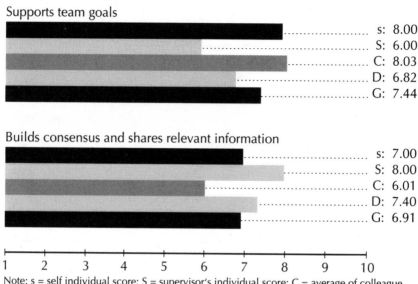

Supports team goals

s: 8.00
S: 6.00
C: 8.03
D: 6.82
G: 7.44

Builds consensus and shares relevant information

s: 7.00
S: 8.00
C: 6.01
D: 7.40
G: 6.91

1　2　3　4　5　6　7　8　9　10

Note: s = self individual score; S = supervisor's individual score; C = average of colleague evaluator type scores; D = average of direct report evaluator type scores; G = average of total group's scores.

Conduct Training II: How to Receive Feedback

Training in how to receive feedback focuses on using the reports to ensure that employees know how to interpret the information they are receiving. Participants need to understand how to accept behavior feedback, how behavior feedback differs substantially from other feedback, and, most important, how to use behavior feedback constructively. Training may cover:

- How to receive feedback constructively
- How to apply the model for performance improvement
- What is contained in the reports
- How to interpret results
- How to create and begin a personal action plan
- How to assess continuous learning and improvements

This second training gives participants a review of the process, instructs them on how to interpret their behavior feedback,

Figure 5-8. Narrative comments report.

Ratee: **Charles Lindbergh**
Survey: **ABC Corp. Developmental Assessment 1**   08/31/x5

COMMENTS REPORT
Specific Commentary

Customer Orientation

Charles is very customer oriented. He is very helpful.

*   *   *

Charlie, perhaps you should allow others to help you with some of your customers. It seems that you may over-extend yourself trying to meet their needs.

*   *   *

WOULD BEND OVER BACKWARDS TO HELP A CUSTOMER

Job Knowledge

Mr. Lindbergh needs to further his education so he can expand his job knowledge more.

*   *   *

Very knowledgeable about his job, but may want to know a little about what the rest of his co-workers do. Cross-training is very valuable.

Planning and Organizing

NOT A VERY ORGANIZED PERSON

*   *   *

Charlie is very organized . . . thanks to his support staff!! If it wasn't for them he would be in quite a mess.

*   *   *

Needs to improve his organizational skills. It seems that his subordinates are always bailing him out of tough situations!

General Commentary

Overall, Charlie is a very well-respected member of our organization. He can be counted on to help out in any situation. He is very dedicated to his customers and his coworkers.—J. Smith

*   *   *

Mr. Lindbergh is a wonderful person to work with. He is a great asset to ABC Corporation.

Figure 5-9. Format for creating an action plan.

PERSONAL ACTION PLAN—BUILDING ON A STRENGTH	
OBJECTIVE What is the targeted strength? What specifically do I want to accomplish?	
STRATEGY / RESOURCES How am I going to achieve the objective and what resources will I need?	
TARGET DATE When will I achieve the objective?	
OBSERVABLE / MEASURABLE RESULTS How will I know I have achieved the objective?	

and helps them understand the information. At least 30 minutes of this 2- to 3-hour training should be devoted to user questions and answers.

Create Action Plans

The feedback highlights areas of strength and areas ripe for development. Action planning means developing a plan for making personal improvements based on this feedback. This is an ongoing process and must be continually reinforced and updated.

The form shown in Figure 5-9 is useful for creating an action plan. The process usually includes sharing the action plan and assessing progress with a supervisor or the work team. Some organizations create support systems, such as employee or career development processes, that offer suggestions for continuous learning and professional development opportunities.

Use of Development Recommendations

Some multisource programs provide computerized development recommendations based on the 360° feedback rather than leaving such actions to the employee. Development recommendations coach employees by specifying which actions they should take. Very little research exists on the value that is added from computer-based generic development recommendations. The following questions guide the use of development recommendations:

- How do users feel about development recommendations made *for* them rather than *by* them?
- How do computer-generated development recommendations affect employee self-responsibility for their own development?
- Do many people get the same development recommendations?
- Do many people get the same development recommendations year after year?
- On how many development recommendations can a person reasonably expect to take action?
- Do computer-generated development recommendations motivate behavior change more than actions plans developed by the individual employee?

There are alternatives to automatic development recommendations:

- Train supervisors on coaching skills using behavior feedback.
- Train employees in peer coaching.
- Have available books or other resources with development recommendations.
- Use support groups to help with the creation of developmental actions.
- Create a development resource guide based on resources available within the organization.

Figure 5-10. Development and training resources guide.

ABC Gas & Oil — Personal Growth Actions: Resources for Development	1. Bias for Action	2. Does it Right the First Time	3. Improves the Process	4. Solves Problems	5. Makes Decisions Effectively	6. Promotes Shared Leadership	7. Credits Others	8. Is an Active Listener	9. Anticipates and Resolves Conflict	10. Minimizes Interpersonal Tension	11. Projects a Positive Impression	12. Communicates Effectively	13. Offers Expertise	14. Takes Responsibility	15. Builds Skills	16. Is Dependable	17. Acts as a Safety Role Model	18. Builds Trust	19. Develops People	20. Coaches for Exceptional Performance	21. Communicates Plans	22. Is Available and Approachable	23. Empowers People
TRAINING RESOURCES																							
Advanced Leadership Practices - Teamwork		X			X	X			X	X		X	X					X		X	X		X
Conflict Resolution				X					X	X	X		X					X	X	X			
Effective Leadership Practices	X	X		X	X	X			X	X		X	X	X				X	X	X		X	X
Effective Negotiating											X				X								
Finance for Nonfinancial Managers													X										
Leadership & Human Relations - Social Styles											X							X	X				
Managing Management Time	X		X															X					X
New Supervisor Orientation	X					X									X		X						
Oil and Gas Accounting													X										
Productivity Plus: Power Meetings													X										
Productivity Plus: Time Management														X	X								
Professional Presentations													X										
Technical Writing													X										
(Leadership) The Journey Continues						X												X	X				X
Transformational Leadership						X												X	X				X

It may be helpful to give employees suggestions for action planning tied to particular competencies. Figure 5-10 shows a development resource guide created by a medium-sized oil and gas company. The training programs and resources listed along the left axis are available within the organizations. The core competencies, across the top, represent the success factors associated with effective performance. For example, the Transformational Leadership program supports competencies around "Promotes Shared Leadership," "Builds Trust," "Develops People," and "Empowers People."

Ensuring Successful Implementation

Organizations must make many decisions and follow a number of steps to ensure a successful implementation of the 360° feedback process. Process implementation, whether as a pilot or an ongoing project, should be followed by analysis of 360° feedback system safeguards and a user assessment, which quickly indicate the quality of the project.

6

Evaluating the 360° Feedback Process

You can see a lot by observing.

—Yogi Berra

Body swayed to the music. O brightening glance,
How can we know the dancer from the dance?

—William Butler Yeats

When employees have started to develop actions plans based on their 360° feedback, an organization may think that the process is over. It is not. In fact, the most critical phase for long-term process success has just begun. The design team or the project administrator needs to examine process safeguards and to allow users to evaluate the process. The organization will want to know if the process met the design team objectives and served stakeholders—especially the employees, management, and the organization—well.

This third and final phase of implementation consists of analyzing safeguards, gaining insight from participants, and developing recommendations to improve the process for the next round of evaluations.

Analyze Safeguards

An effective 360° feedback system predictably yields relatively low scores for some participants. Those with low scores often become defensive and may attack the entire process. Safeguards help defend the system and validate feedback results. Typically, users have these concerns:

- What if someone purposely and unfairly rated me extremely low?
- What if some respondents used intentionally unfair rating strategies?
- What if someone read the scale backward? (It happens!)
- What happens to obviously invalid responses?
- Does the distribution of behavior feedback scores reflect advantage to any organizational or demographic group?
- What if my evaluation team was, by chance, more rigorous than others?

Safeguard Analysis

Organizations can evaluate safeguards to determine if the 360° feedback process met the intended goals. Technology safeguards, created by computer, analyze the response pattern to examine anomalies or variations from expected patterns. Safeguard evaluation helps pinpoint where problems may have occurred.

Safeguard Reports

Safeguard reports, created by well-designed software, can provide in-depth information about the process. (Figure 6-1 offers descriptions of various safeguard reports.) Safeguards indicate immediately if a 360° feedback project is not effective because respondent behaviors show what people thought about the process. For example, in a successful project, the item (survey question) response rate is high—greater than 85 percent—which means most people responded to most items. When users do not support a multisource process, response rates will be low.

Intercorrelation among items and factor analysis examine the response pattern to determine which items, if any, people responded to in the same way. A similar response pattern among two items—a correlation above .80 for example—indicates that respondents viewed the content of those two items similarly. For example, two very different questions about safety behavior may be

(text continues on page 130)

Figure 6-1. Guide to safeguards.

Name	What It Does	How It is Used
Item response rate	Shows a count of responses.	Identifies items to which people did not respond. May show instrument is too long if many nonresponses occur in the second half of the instrument.
Item reliability or respondent agreement	Shows degree of respondent agreement or spread of ratings on each item.	Identifies items to which people had difficulty responding consistently with others. May indicate nonreliable or nonunderstood items.
Item reliability by respondent type	Shows degree of respondent agreement on each item by type of respondent (e.g., colleagues).	May indicate items that should not be rated by this respondent type; item reliability is especially interesting when run by organization level, age, gender, or ethnicity.
Intercorrelation among items	Relates correspondence among survey questions.	Identifies items to which people responded similarly. May indicate redundant items.
Factor analysis	Relates correspondence among survey questions and groups of questions.	Identifies items to which people responded similarly. May indicate redundant items.
Response distribution	Shows the distribution of responses for each item and across all items.	Identifies items to which people responded unusually high or low. May indicate difficulty in responding. Trust is a construct that often is nearly uniformly high (dependability, for example, shows a consistently wider distribution of ratings than trust).

Name	What It Does	How It is Used
Rating scale distribution	Shows the percentage of ratings for each number on the rating scale and the number of nonresponses.	Shows rater behavior and may identify scale inflation.
Ratings scale distribution by respondent type	Shows the percentage of ratings for each number on the rating scale by different perspectives.	Shows rater behavior by perspective. Answers questions like: Did colleagues or direct reports rate higher? May show useful information for rater training when run by demographic variables.
Score distribution	Shows how many participants received scores within defined ranges.	Shows score distribution and may provide useful diversity analysis when created by demographic variables, e.g., gender.
Score distribution by organizational level	Shows how many participants at each organization level received scores within defined ranges.	May provide useful information regarding hierarchy (level) bias. Nearly all assessment methods result in higher scores for people higher in the organization hierarchy.
Respondents > 20 percent different from others (or > 30 percent or any other level)	Shows respondents whose response pattern is significantly different from others.	Identifies respondents who may be making unintentional or intentional rating errors.
Reciprocal inflated scores	Shows combinations of respondents who rated one another very high.	May indicate respondent collusion.
Evaluation team rigor	Compares the relative rigor of each evaluation team.	Answers the question: Was my evaluation team by chance more difficult than others?

rated the same because respondents tend to clump safety into one behavior set. Although redundant questions are unnecessary in 360° feedback systems, similar questions may be retained in order to communicate important competencies. For example, when one Intel facility found that the two safety questions were redundant in a statistical response sense, they decided to ask four questions about safety in order to emphasize the importance of safety.

In successful projects, item reliability in total and by respondent type will be high. The response distribution shows if respondents took their responsibility seriously or simply used the top-of-the rating scale and provided inflated scores. The other measures of rating scale and score distribution identify more specifically the sources of reliable or unreliable scores.

A key to data integrity is a response measure that examines respondent variations that are more than 20 percent different from others. For example, when someone rates another unfairly, that response pattern stands out as significantly different from the others. Although trimmed mean scoring removes the impact of these anomalies, it is important to know how often they occur. A good project will have fewer than 5 percent of respondents who are significantly different from others.

In science, a significant difference is typically 20 percent, so the respondent variation from other respondent parameters may be set at 20 percent. Some organizations create a respondent validity policy with more rigorous measures (e.g., 15 percent difference) or more lenient ones (e.g., 30 percent different). A respondent validity policy may state that a respondent who is more than 30 percent different from all other respondents over 30 percent of the time is invalid. The probability of this person's being right and all others wrong this often is negligible. The respondent validity policy may require that this respondent be removed from process scoring. Some organizations even refer such respondents to their ethics and compliance process. Once respondents are aware that when they try to game the system, they will both lose their voice in the process and be identified, integrity increases.

The analysis of response patterns can also be used to identify reciprocally inflated respondents, which may indicate collusion among respondents. The response pattern of people who decide to give one another largely inflated scores is obvious from this type of report.

The determination of evaluation team rigor is also important because it identifies whether any evaluation team was substantially tougher or more lenient than others. A team composed of respondents who all tended to use the low part of the rating scale for most of the people they rated would yield an unusually rigorous evaluation team measure. This type of report also can identify collusion among respondents. Most commonly this report reinforces the fact that most people responded honestly and that nearly all evaluation teams (97 percent) are about equal in their composition of extremely rigorous and lenient respondents.

Other safeguards may reveal an effective 360° feedback process:

- A high percentage (more than 80 percent) of requested respondents responded.
- A high percentage (more than 95 percent) of participating employees have sufficient data to receive reports.
- A majority of respondents used the scale effectively (e.g., they used a 4-point spread or more on the 10-point scale).
- Interrater agreement was high (more than 70 percent agreement).
- There was a low set of highly inconsistent responses (less than 5 percent of respondents with more than 20 percent difference from the consensus of others).
- There was a low set of respondents (less than 5 percent who used predominantly the top or bottom of the scale).

Some organizations change the parameters associated with respondent accuracy and validity, such as the percentage agreement or the percentage of inconsistent responses, in order to set higher standards for data integrity.

Respondent Concerns

How well did the organization meet the needs and concerns of respondents? If users do not trust the 360° feedback process to preserve their anonymity as respondents, many do not respond, and those who do tend to inflate their responses. If users feel the instrument is too long or they must fill out too many because evaluation teams are too large, the percentage of nonresponses increases substantially. In addition, those who do respond will tend to show little variation in use of the scale. If they feel they are asked to provide feedback for people they do not know sufficiently, they will either not respond or respond with nearly all similar, usually slightly above midscale, ratings.

Instrument Safeguards

Does the survey or assessment instrument result in reliable and valid assessments? A valid instrument will have:

- High interrater agreement for each item (criterion, competency, or question)
- High response rate for each item (better than 90 percent response) and
- Few redundant items, indicated by low or modest intercorrelation with other items

Respondent Accuracy

Did stakeholders respond in a pattern typical of their group? Generally organizations find similar response patterns within each respondent category; for example, self-ratings tend to be inflated, and external customers tend to provide higher ratings than internal customers. The analysis of accuracy, defined as consistency with various other respondent types, assists with policy decisions. This analysis can help project administrators decide which respondent types to use in the future and whether to use differential weighting of respondent types. Different weightings of various respondent types, such as colleagues or direct reports, can substantially influence composite or summary scores.

Respondent Feedback

Respondent feedback, a special safeguard that creates accountability for respondent accuracy, is based on the concept that

Figure 6-2. Respondent feedback report.

Respondent: CHARLES LINDBERGH

RESPONDENT FEEDBACK REPORT — **EVALUATED ON:** Performance

SURVEY: ABC Corp. Developmental Assessment # 1 — 5/03/x4

	Crit#:	1	2	3	4	5	6	7	8	9	10	11	12	13	14	15
Wendy Smith		*	L	*	*	*	*	*	*	*	*	–	*	*	*	*
Susan Williams		L	L	*	*	*	*	*	*	*	*	–	*	*	*	*
David C. Canfield		*	*	*	*	*	*	*	*	*	*	*	*	*	*	*
John Hanover		*	*	*	*	H	*	H	H	*	*	*	H	*	*	*

John Hanover is one of the feedback receivers that Charles Lindbergh evaluated.

*On crit. #2, Charles' evaluation of Susan was more than 20% **lower** than the average score Susan received.*

*On crit. #7, Charles' evaluation of John was more than 20% **higher** than the average score John Hanover received.*

Charles did not respond to crit. #11 on his evaluation of Susan.

Totals (% of Total): High 4 (2.0%) Low 10 (8.3%) N/A 3 (2.5%)

*Overall, 2.0% (4 out of 120) of Charles' evaluations were significantly **higher**.*

*Overall, 8.3% (10 out of 120) of Charles' evaluations were significantly **lower**.*

Overall, Charles did not respond to 2.5% (3 out of 120) evaluation questions.

valid respondents do what they are supposed to do: provide feedback consistently with others. Invalid respondents may be identified as those whose response pattern is greater than 20 percent different from other respondents over 40 percent of the time, although some organizations widen or narrow the parameters in this definition.

Respondent feedback ensures all participants that the feedback process is fair. Although respondents are accountable for accuracy, their anonymity is preserved. The person receiving 360° feedback *never* sees the respondent feedback for others. It goes only to the feedback provider and sometimes to the human resources department. Therefore, the person who is rated never sees who was in or out of bounds in their responses.

Many people have made performance judgments about employees and wondered if they were on or off target. Respondent feedback shows respondents where their own judgments differed substantially from the consensus of others (Figure 6-2). Respondent feedback can both reinforce valid respondents and identify invalid respondents.

The respondent feedback report in Figure 6-2 was created for the evaluator, Charles Lindbergh. He provided feedback for four people: Wendy Smith, Susan Williams, David Canfield, and John Hanover. In responding to the instrument for Susan Williams, the L indicates that Charles was more than 20 percent lower than the consensus of other respondents on the first to criteria (questions). This does not mean he was wrong in his assessment. He may have seen Susan in different situations than the others. However, if he had rated Susan on many items substantially different from others, he probably would be wrong.

Charles did not provide feedback for Susan on criterion 11. When providing feedback for John Hanover, Charles was substantially higher than the other respondents on four criteria (indicated by H).

The totals of low, high, and no ratings indicate Charles was a fairly good respondent. Respondent validity comes into question when the total of unusually high or low responses exceed 20 percent of all responses. Respondent feedback flags a concern if, for example, Susan Williams had received all L ratings, indicating probable person bias. Similarly, if a respondent were to rate all women or any other identifiable group unusually low, this report would flag the occurrence.

Exactly how this information should be used is a policy decision, often made by the feedback design team. Most often, the policy is to eliminate the ratings from an obviously invalid respondent because they create unfair distortion to the information. Sometimes the respondent validity policy is stronger, and those who do not respond honestly are exposed to their colleagues.

Respondent feedback also provides a test of item reliability. For example, if multiple respondents were high or low on the same item, perhaps they needed a better definition of the construct.

Few people have ever previously received feedback about the accuracy of their judgments about others, except possibly from their spouse or significant other. Most of those who receive respondent feedback are delighted, and possibly relieved, when their judgment matches others. Respondent feedback is welcome for most people. In fact, participants at Arizona Public Service, Current, Inc., Fidelity Bank, and du Pont reported that respondent feedback was the most valuable element of the 360° feedback process.

Feedback on specific errors that occur during assessments, such as the tendency to use only the top end of the rating scale—leniency—or the center of the scale—central tendency—or other errors provides excellent respondent training by experiential learning. Respondent feedback allows participants to learn by experience in the process of providing feedback. For most respondents, the evaluation experience is positive because their judgments are validated by the similar assessments by others. For those who rate others unfairly, respondent feedback can serve as a wake-up call to change their behavior as a respondent.

Respondent feedback motivates respondents to change their rating behavior to avoid errors. This feedback also can illustrate possible favorable or unfavorable bias to individuals or to groups. For example, the feedback for a person who rates a friend consistently at the top of the scale and a nonfriend at the bottom is obvious. Similarly, respondent feedback identifies those who rate women or any other identifiable group substantially different for others.

When respondents collude and create a rating ring or cabal, their feedback exposes and documents this inappropriate behavior. The footprint of those who collude becomes obvious. Without the ability to identify and intervene when respondents collude, more collusion will quickly happen, which will undermine the integrity of the results.

A University Creates Sanctions for Respondents Who Collude

A major university's 360° feedback project resulted in the identification of three professors, two tenured and one not, who tried to "game the system" to their favor. They were not only invalid respondents, but they also colluded by creating a cabal or rating ring, rating each other consistently to the maximum over all evaluation criteria and all others consistently at the minimum. They knew from their training that the system would track and report rater responses to guard against invalidity but nevertheless went ahead with their plan.

When their behavior was exposed by the respondent feedback

that clearly showed their behavior from their response pattern, they at first claimed innocence. Once they were shown the evidence from their behavior feedback reports, each said: "I thought everybody was doing it."

The personnel committee had a different opinion of their colleagues who had clearly cheated the rest of the faculty: They created a policy that made invalid respondents ineligible for providing feedback for the next two process iterations. The committee also recommended the professors be denied merit increases. All three professors voluntarily left the university within two years.

Respondents who try to manipulate the 360° feedback assessment process to their favor may be:

- Removed from scoring (so they essentially lose their voice in the process)
- Exposed through the documentation
- Recommended for honesty or diversity training
- Subject to ethics and compliance sanctions, if such exist

Some respondent deviation from others is normal and desired. Different perspectives, for example, are expected to create variations in behavior observation. Invalidity occurs when the pattern of deviations is obviously groundless, such as rating one person or one group of people all to the top or bottom of the scale when others do not.

A High-Tech Service Firm Breaks Up a Rating Ring

A high-tech organization examined respondent feedback and realized that a group of about eight people had colluded and rated each other uniformly at the top of the rating scale. When those who had intentionally provided invalid feedback were confronted, most said: "I thought everyone was doing it [cheating]."

The organization elected to give these employees a second chance to be honest. It also decided to reveal that a rater ring had been found, though it did not report the names, and it reported that those who participated had not gained advantage.

In the future, anyone caught providing invalid feedback or colluding with others in any assessment process would be subject to the rigorous ethics and compliance policy that calls for high integrity in the workplace and included provision for disciplinary action and even discharge for employees who acted in a clearly unethical manner.

Respondent feedback serves as a safeguard to ensure fairness by holding respondents accountable for honest feedback. Since the subject, the person rated, does not see the respondent feedback, respondent anonymity is preserved. Without respondent feedback, assessments are likely to be contaminated by substantial unintentional and intentional invalid ratings.

Organizational Roll-up Reports

Group-level or full organization roll-up reports offer both safeguards and additional process information. A roll-up report combines the individual 360° feedback reports from a department, for example, to create a department average. They can be used to determine training and development needs, measure training effectiveness, gauge cultural change, and check alignment of organizational behaviors and values.

Roll-up reports by demographic variables provide valuable insight into how assessments affect particular groups, such as how women scored compared with men or one ethnicity compared with any or all others. In anticipation of user questions, safeguards can provide answers to the questions like: "Does my job family of engineering score higher or lower as a group than another job family, like marketing?" Safeguards can identify score differences, if they exist for various variable such as age, education, or length of service. The following demographic variables are useful for roll-up or aggregate reports:

- job or job family
- organization level
- geographic location
- length of employment in the organization
- length of employment in the job

- education
- age
- gender
- ethnicity

Organizations can use roll-up information for reengineering, reorganizing, succession planning, placement, and other selection decision processes. For example, the department roll-ups indicate where targeted training may be needed. When an organization requires a set of employees who have strong customer service and teamwork competencies, it can query the database to select a group demonstrating those targeted skills most strongly.

Conduct User Assessments

The most common method of gaining information about process effectiveness is user satisfaction surveys. An organization can conduct a user survey to evaluate the 360° feedback process for fairness, accuracy, and other attributes important to the organization and its employees. The short assessment shown in Figure 6-3 may be used to analyze process effectiveness.

MERIDIAN OIL CONDUCTS A STRUCTURED 360° FEEDBACK PROCESS ASSESSMENT

Meridian Oil sent an evaluation survey to 1,800 recent users of the 360° feedback process at six sites across North America. Over 1,000 people responded; the results are shown in Figure 6-4. Most users— about 78 percent—felt the assessment provided useful information. About 15 percent were neutral, and about 4 percent disagreed with the statement that the 360° feedback process provided useful information. The least disagreement occurred on the statement: "The process is fair." Evidently very few users were not impressed with the process fairness.

Demographic analysis showed that employees of varying ages, genders, and ethnic backgrounds shared very similar, positive perceptions about the feedback process. The results were consistent with other postproject assessments that showed supervisors were slightly more positive than nonsupervisory employees.

Meridian Oil asked employees their opinion about moving the process from developmental-only feedback to one that would affect

Figure 6-3. Project assessment instrument.

Don't Know	Strongly Disagree		Disagree				Agree		Strongly Agree	
N	1	2	3	4	5	6	7	8	9	10

The new 360° feedback process provides me with information that:

1. Is useful for
   development.................. N 1 2 3 4 5 6 7 8 9 10
2. Is useful for appraisal ..... N 1 2 3 4 5 6 7 8 9 10
3. Motivates me................ N 1 2 3 4 5 6 7 8 9 10
4. Is valuable for me .... N 1 2 3 4 5 6 7 8 9 10
5. Is fair to me................... N 1 2 3 4 5 6 7 8 9 10
6. Is fair to others............... N 1 2 3 4 5 6 7 8 9 10
7. Is a complete
   assessment................... N 1 2 3 4 5 6 7 8 9 10
8. Is an accurate
   assessment................... N 1 2 3 4 5 6 7 8 9 10
9. Provides safeguards for
   fairness .... N 1 2 3 4 5 6 7 8 9 10
10. Overall, I am satisfied
    with the 360° process .... N 1 2 3 4 5 6 7 8 9 10

11. Comments:

_____

_____

_____

_____

What would you like to change most on the survey?

_____

_____

_____

_____

I prefer to receive feedback from:
_____ My supervisor only
_____ My coworkers only
_____ Both my supervisor and my coworkers

Overall, I recommend using 360° feedback for:
_____ For performance evaluation in 1996 (now)
_____ For performance evaluation in 1997 (next year)
_____ Using 360° feedback for developmental purposes only

Figure 6-4. Meridian Oil's process assessment results.

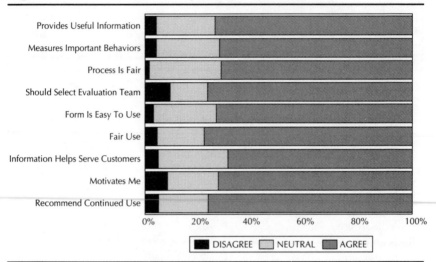

appraisal and pay decisions. If most employees view the 360° feedback process as fair and recommend continued use, what should be expected if they are asked if the 360° feedback process should support appraisal and pay? At Meridian Oil, as shown in Figure 6-5, the majority of employees—85 percent—recommended the 360° feedback process be used for appraisal and pay. Still, 44 percent thought the use of the process for pay should be put off a year, and 14 percent recommended that the process not be used for pay. The responses were nearly the same across demographic categories.

Organizations also can examine the effectiveness of a 360° feedback process by comparing a pretest with a posttest. The pretest measures employee satisfaction with the previous performance evaluation process. Generally, between 5 and 30 percent of employees are satisfied with single-source assessment processes. The posttest, which measures employee satisfaction with the 360° feedback systems, often exceeds 75 percent, although public sector and union membership satisfaction levels may be as much as 15 percent lower.

Figure 6-5. Results of survey of Meridian Oil's employees on using 360° feedback for pay.

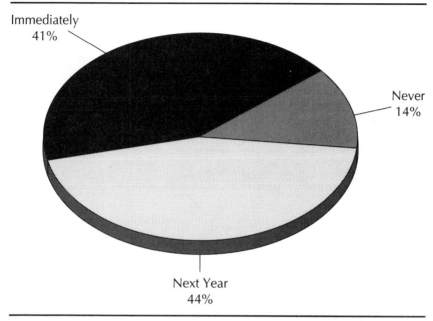

Immediately
41%

Never
14%

Next Year
44%

INTEL FINDS ITS 360° FEEDBACK PROJECT "TASTES GREAT; LESS FILLING"

Intel asked participants thirty-two questions about their perceptions of the 360° feedback process, which is used to support both development and performance appraisal and pay decisions. Two items, shown in Figure 6-6 were critical: Does the process "provide useful information" and is it "time efficient"? Project leaders at Intel dubbed these project attributes, "Tastes great; less filling." It tastes great because it adds value and is less filling because it requires minimal time. Over 90 percent of Intel participants found that 360° feedback provided useful information and was time efficient. In contrast, less than one-third found the prior process either useful or time efficient.

User assessments may not provide sufficient insight into user feelings. The U.S. Department of Energy and OXY USA used interviews, staff meetings, and focus groups to gather additional information about the strengths and concerns users felt about the 360°

Figure 6-6. Process assessment at Intel: Comparing single source and multisource.

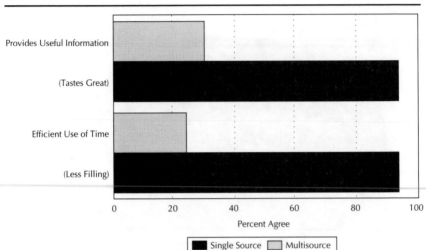

feedback process. Figure 6-7 shows participants' thoughts on du Pont's 360° system after a five-year process assessment. User assessment showed about 88 percent satisfaction with the 360° feedback process that supported development, appraisal, pay, and promotion decisions in the research and development division. The expressed concerns indicate that additional communication was needed to address various process issues.

A self-scoring process assessment, shown in Figure 6-8, offers a quick method for assessing process effectiveness. The target level for user satisfaction, such as 75 percent, means that a successful project will have greater than 75 percent user support.

Refine the 360° Feedback Process

Organizations should use the information gathered from the evaluation to refine the 360° feedback process. If the original process design was strong, process refinements will be minor. The most common modifications are in the following areas:

Figure 6-7.   Assessment at du Pont: Strengths and concerns about 360° feedback from long-term users.

Strengths	Concerns
Creates accurate performance measures in less time	Popularity bias (fairness of each evaluation team)*
Creates credible performance feedback	Friendship or competition bias*
Enables equitable pay for performance	Some respondents more critical than others*
Creates more distinction in performance, a wider spread of scores	Some teams are harder than others*
Communicates critical behaviors	Some people may collude*
Changes from a seniority to a performance system	Measures are too soft (not enough technical skills and outcomes)
Allows rewarding of high performers	Measures are not complete (no results or outcome measures)
Confronts low performers	Process would not support retention decisions
Drives continuous improvement	
Supports team environment	
Supports broad spans of supervision	
Reduces supervisor bias	
Supports career development	

*Solved with respondent tracking and respondent feedback.

- Policy decisions, such as who has access to the behavior feedback
- The instrument itself (e.g., the addition, deletion, or modification of selected constructs or sets of technical or functional skills)
- Evaluation team selection guidelines (usually to broaden participation)
- Process administration (often to speed or simplify user response)
- The addition of safeguards, such as on respondent feedback
- Actions to make the process fair, accurate, simple, trustworthy, or faster

Figure 6-8. Self-scoring 360° project assessment.

Please rate the degree to which the 360° feedback systems supports each statement. Please use a 10-point scale where 10 is high.

	Score (1–10)	Target
1. Users see 360° feedback as valuable.	____	> 75%
2. Users view the process as fair.	____	> 75%
3. High user participation.	____	> 85%
4. Requires a minimum amount of time.	____	< 20 minutes
5. A communications plan was used to educate users.	____	yes
6. A cross-functional design team is involved in the process.	____	yes
7. Users were trained in providing and receiving feedback.	____	yes
8. Policy decisions make sense to users.	____	yes
9. Intelligent scoring is used.	____	yes
10. Process and technology safeguards are used.	____	yes

Scoring

Over 80: Successful project; 360° will be embraced.
60 to 80: Modest success; 360° needs redesign.
Under 60: No success; 360° needs major redesign.

Learn by Doing

The 360° feedback process is much like riding a bicycle. No one can truly learn it by observation alone. Some participants comment that receiving behavior feedback from work associates feels like riding a bicycle naked. The first exposure to 360° feedback is the most difficult for most participants; completing the project quells the predictable speculation about how users will receive this new type of information.

Part III

User Concerns and Needs

7

Common Pitfalls and How to Avoid Them

The ripest peach is highest on the tree.
—Raymond Welch, Jr., farmer

The greatest rewards come only from the greatest commitment.
—Arlene Blum, mountain climber and leader, American Women's Himalayan Expedition

360° feedback offers obvious benefits, yet only a few organizations use this process for appraisal and pay. Among the reasons that this method is not widely used is that most users substantially underestimate the work involved in designing a 360° feedback project. Another is the lack of a good road map that charts a path around the predictable obstacles. Figure 7-1 provides a comparison of 360° feedback with traditional surveys.

Common Pitfalls

An explanation of the pitfalls that commonly undermine the implementation of 360° feedback provides insight into why more organizations have not fully implemented the approach.

Misapplying Old Learning

The number one reason that multisource projects fail is that users try to force the multisource model to comply with their existing

Figure 7-1. Traditional surveys and 360° feedback:
a comparison.

Traditional Surveys	360° Feedback or Multisource Assessment
One target, many respondents (large sample, e.g., more than 15)	Many targets, each with a few respondents (small sample, e.g., 4 to 9)
Classic inferential statistics hold	Sample is size too small to meet statistical assumptions; statistical tests may be invalid
Classic reports are appropriate, such as showing respondent distribution	May not want to show respondent distribution since a low rating may negatively motivate the feedback receiver
No need for specialized scoring, sample size moderates distortion (good input washes out the bad or invalid)	May need to use a trimmed mean to stabilize the score due to an outlier
Modest need for respondent anonymity	Critical need for respondent anonymity
Instruments may be long because each respondent completes one instrument	Instruments must be short because most respondents complete multiple instruments
Few safeguards are necessary due to large sample size	Safeguards to fairness are required due to use and to small sample size and how the results will be used

knowledge, such as traditional survey research. Simple survey methods may work fine for development-only feedback (although arguably with problems), but they are substantially deficient for performance management. A simple survey method for scoring and reporting will give some users predictably distorted information because of respondent or technology errors, or both.

Users often apply what they know about traditional surveys to the specialized model associated with 360° feedback systems because the two processes appear to be very similar. In fact, traditional survey processes are as different from 360° feedback as a propeller aircraft is different from a jet.

A traditional opinion survey administered to 1,000 employees, for example, means there is one target, the organization, with a large sample of 1,000 respondents. The 360° feedback model is almost the inverse: there are 1,000 targets, one for each employee and each with a small, unique respondent group of four to nine people. The small sample has substantial implications for the scoring and reporting needed to create accurate feedback. Standard statistical methods may not be appropriate to small sample sizes because the assumptions behind their use are broken.

Traditional survey systems assume a reasonable sample size, so one response has little impact on the mean of many responses. In contrast, without scoring safeguards in a 360° feedback sample, one respondent may have a significant impact on the mean.

Traditional surveys can use long surveys because respondents answer only once. In contrast, users typically answer five to twelve 360° feedback surveys. If a long survey is used for 360° feedback, it will yield many nonrespondents and probably largely spurious results. People are willing to think about themselves when answering a long set of questions in a self-assessment but generally are not as willing to give serious thought about their colleagues for a lengthy period of time.

Large sample surveys allow respondents to blend in with many other respondents. Hence, there is only a modest need for anonymity. Anonymity, as we have seen, is critical for effective 360° systems or respondents will not be honest.

Lack of Safeguards

Too often organizations approach the 360° feedback process assuming that using information from more sources will compensate for intentional and unintentional respondent distortion. It does not. *When collected incorrectly, information from multiple sources increases rather than reduces error.* Failure to account for unintentional and intentional rating errors destroys the credibility of assessment results.

The validity of process administration may be more important than the validity of the assessment instrument. A valid process administration requires that feedback providers are trained and guaranteed anonymity for their evaluations. It also means that the individual feedback reports are confidential and that other employees do not have access to the information.

Safeguards help an organization prepare for and correct any errors that may occur during the 360° feedback process. These process and technology safeguards must be in place and then evaluated for effectiveness for each use of the process.

Overreliance on Technology

The 360° feedback model uses multiple respondents, which makes it look like a technology challenge. Many people mistakenly believe that software to facilitate process administration solves the challenge. Certainly technology is important, but the process side—for example, how the process is communicated, the credibility of the survey, the training on how to provide and receive feedback, and how to create action plans—has a lot more to do with user acceptance than the software used to score results.

Yet overreliance on technology occurs repeatedly as organizations install or outsource a process to collect and score surveys without creating the necessary support systems to help people understand the process and how to use the results. Failure to manage the mechanics will foil the 360° feedback project, but attention to this aspect alone is insufficient. Successful projects include both strong process and technology support.

Substituting Labor for Technology

An initial, small 360° feedback project can be delegated to a clerical person to administer; however, without efficient application software, coordinating the process quickly becomes far too difficult. Many organizations, such as Current, Inc., American Airlines, and Kaiser Permanente, initially used people instead of technology before they migrated to automated technology solutions. Others terminated their projects because the process, without adequate automated technology, required far too much administrative time.

Home-Grown Technology

The 360° feedback process appears so easy that many people think they can use a spreadsheet or database scoring process. An agro-chemical company invested several hundred thousand dollars on internally developed multisource assessment software before dropping the project because the challenge was too difficult. West-inghouse and Ciba-Geigy had a similar experience. Companies have made large investments in creating computer programs, which turned out to have such limited use that they dropped the programs.

Homemade applications may work when introducing multi-source assessment, especially when used for development-only feedback and in small groups. However, as users become more sophisticated, they want additional features that are likely to be beyond the capacity of a simple home-grown computer program. Consequently, the investment in in-house-created technology must recur regularly to keep up with user needs and improvements in computer technologies.

Administrative Overhead

Any significant change in an organization requires an internal champion to orchestrate the project. Additionally, leaders and su-pervisors must support the project, and the organization should designate a person to be in charge of the project. When no one has the responsibility for program administration, the system will fail.

Administrative support should include:

- A *process administrator*, responsible for the design, implemen-tation, and maintenance of the process.
- A *clerical person*, charged with the responsibilities of han-dling the paper or technology flow, notifying people who did not respond, and attending to administrative detail, such as sending additional surveys to people who have lost them.
- *Area coordinators*, with the responsibility to ensure that each participant has selected an evaluation team and that each team member has returned an evaluation form to the coordi-

nator. Typically the coordinator needs to follow up with 10 to 20 percent of participants who are delinquent.

An objection frequently raised when administrative support is requested is that the process is too complex to administer efficiently. This objection can be overcome by piloting a 360° feedback process to demonstrate the simplicity of each administrative activity. Taken together, all of these administrative activities require a relatively modest investment of time and resources. Automation can substantially reduce administrative support needs. For example, changing from paper surveys to an automated, online system enables one system administrator to support up to two thousand users.

Culture Shock

Any process that requires a cultural change is difficult to introduce and complete successfully. Highly autocratic, hierarchical organizations are difficult candidates for 360° feedback. Conversely, an organization whose vision, values, and leadership truly support empowerment, teamwork, and continuous improvement offer an excellent launching point.

Two tightly controlled and hierarchically driven manufacturing companies created multisource assessment processes out of employee rebellion to strict managerial control. Employees were tired of the politics and cronyism and demanded more voice in the quality of their leadership. Four years later, one organization has leaders who champion the new values of employee participation. In the other one, the supervisors unilaterally ended the multisource "experiment" to reclaim control of their supervisory power. Multisource assessments may fail when they represent too great a change from the existing leadership norm.

The two-part TEAMS model discussed previously is an effective way to introduce 360° feedback in these environments. A 360° feedback component may initially serve as an advisory input to supervisors, who can augment this information by documenting specific results. The TEAMS model thus allows a balance between the 360° feedback process and the supervisor's assessment of results. It protects employees who have responsibilities or accomplishments that are not known or observable to anyone other than the immediate supervisor, and it involves the supervisor in both segments of the evaluation process: the behavioral assessment and the results component. Users are more willing to support adoption when they have become comfortable with the new approach through incremental implementation.

Autocracy

Organizations with autocratic senior managers tend to be highly resistant to even considering 360° feedback. These managers achieved their organizational rank under the old rules of supervisor-only evaluations and can be reluctant to change the rules in any fashion that could pose a threat to their positions of power.

The autocratic style of management, which typically relies on high control by senior management, does not foster support in employee participation in the performance feedback and measurement process. An airline that attempted to use multisource assessment in an autocratic management group found the loss-of-control problem was too much for managers. Although project assessment results indicated 88 percent of employees supported the multisource process and management support was 82 percent, one highly autocratic, and highly threatened, senior manager served as a gatekeeper and unilaterally terminated the process.

Even in participative organizations that move to 360° feedback, a few autocratic managers may be substantial opponents of the process. They may feel far more comfortable when they are in control of the decision system that determines employee rewards. Often these managers will willingly state their preference that assessment and accountability occur "to them" and not "to me."

The most effective way around autocratic obstacles is an incremental approach. First, find one or more leaders or groups who are leaning toward employee empowerment who will participate in 360° feedback pilot. After a successful pilot, more leaders and employees are willing to jump on the bandwagon and try the new process. In autocratic, hierarchically driven organizations, the best way to implement 360° feedback may be bottom up. Once employees adopt the new culture, managers are likely to follow.

Cronyism

During implementation, project administrators are likely to come across employees who have reached their position through cronyism. Sometimes these political favorites are relatively mediocre performers who provide little threat to the senior managers. In these situations, cronyism rewards mediocrity and provides a disincentive for high performance, due to the potential for threatening the position or confidence of the immediate supervisor.

The 360° feedback process threatens to eliminate cronyism, thus putting cronies in grave danger. No longer can managers arbitrarily reward political favorites and mediocre performers. Truly high-performing employees are likely to be accurately identified as the high contributors as a result of 360° feedback. Managers then will have to distribute rewards according to performance rather than politics.

In organizations controlled by cronies, those in positions of power have a high incentive to maintain the existing political reward structure and to undermine 360° feedback systems. The risk of losing their hard-earned political power can lead to fierce struggles to maintain the status quo. Therefore, 360° systems must be designed carefully to diffuse the predictable attacks on the process and credibility. When cronyism is a challenge, the best strategy may be a bottom-up implementation plan.

Nepotism

Nepotism too can undermine a 360° feedback project. In a large multinational, privately owned food company that employed many family members, the process yielded information that accurately reflected the high, medium, and low performers. Nevertheless, the politics of nepotism defeated the 360° feedback process because family members felt threatened.

Some family members—about one-third—were high performers and were rated as doing an excellent job by their colleagues. But the feedback also showed that some family members were poor performers and that many of them were in jobs above their level of training and experience. Exposing these family members as mediocre performers was unacceptable to senior management, many of whom shared the family name. Consequently, the company dropped the 360° feedback in favor of traditional supervisor-only assessment systems so family members could continue to shelter their relatives.

User surveys showing process support by a majority of employees and managers can overcome the effects of a relatively few nay-sayers—whether the concern is nepotism or another problem.

Coasters

Some organizations have a relatively large number of senior organization members who occupy space and use organization resources but have long since ceased to be productive. These coasters also are known as deadwood, in-place retired, and window watchers. At a large service company they are called empty suits and at a manufacturing company, wasted shoes. By whatever name, they try to block the use of any credible performance feedback systems because their nonperformance will be exposed. People who have chosen to retire on the job know that an accurate appraisal system does not serve their best interests. If these people have high organizational positions and substantial political influence, they can mount substantial opposition to a new evaluation system.

Like cronies, coasters have strong incentives to ensure that 360° feedback does not expose them. In a manufacturing company, one senior manager who felt very threatened by the new process announced that it would be used in the organization only "over his dead body." Nevertheless, the project went forward, and the 360° feedback results confirmed what everyone already knew: this manager's secretary was doing his work. Initially, he tried every logical and spurious argument against the process. When the implementers methodically answered every objection, he shifted his position: He accepted the feedback that told him that he was not serving his internal or external customers and began taking the actions necessary to perform. Ultimately he became a strong contributor. He then left the company two years later for a substantial promotion at another organization. His first act in his new assignment? He initiated a 360° feedback process.

Betrayal of Employee Trust

When organizations decide to use 360° feedback, they must inform employees of its intended use and then stick with this plan. A large high-technology company piloted a multisource assessment, saying the results would be used for career development and training. But when it faced a reduction in force and needed information to decide which employees would be kept and which would not, management decided to use the results of the feedback process.

Employees naturally became enraged that the team evaluation information was used for purposes other than those intended. The uproar over the betrayal of trust was so significant that management curtailed all evaluations. Ironically, many employees reported later that they would have supported the process for reduction in force and even agreed to the use of previously gathered multisource information—if they had been asked for approval before the information was used.

Supervisor Inaction

Multisource systems fail when supervisors neglect their responsibilities for performance feedback. At one law firm, lawyers evaluated other staff members—legal secretaries, paralegals, typists, and so on—but many of these lawyer supervisors were too busy to discuss the evaluation results. Naturally, staff members became frustrated with the whole evaluation process.

In a surprising number of organizations, many employees are not experienced in either giving or receiving performance feedback. If top management allows this situation to occur, management and employees ignore the feedback process, pretending it does not exist. Although managers are paid to manage, many prefer to escape the tough task of providing feedback and coaching performance.

Supervisors often think they give performance feedback and coaching, yet they may present the feedback in such a manner that the direct reports cannot identify it. An employee may say she has not had a performance review in six years, yet her supervisor will attest to conducting performance reviews on an ongoing basis. Obviously, the communication is inadequate.

A benefit of 360° feedback is that the results are documented. The report is relevant and clear. Therefore, even when a supervisor provides no additional feedback or coaching, the employee has quality performance information from 360° feedback.

Training

Organizations too often forget the importance of training, yet problems occur when employees and supervisors have no training in performance feedback. Many supervisors avoid the feedback process or provide nearly useless information to direct reports. And employees who are given negative behavior feedback, from a multisource system or any other evaluative procedure, will find the evaluation process distasteful.

A chemical manufacturer introduced 360° feedback to the organization without any employee training. The result was that many employees were devastated because the results were far more rigorous than expected, and others were outright confused. Employees need help in learning how to receive, understand, and use behavior feedback.

Two actions improve the quality of supervisor input in the performance feedback process, specifically to 360° feedback. One is training to supervisors on how to coach employees. The other is to ask direct reports to rate the supervisor's skills in performance coaching. A leader who gets feedback from a number of direct reports that his or her performance feedback is deficient will be motivated to take action to improve skills in this area.

Anonymity and Confidentiality

360° feedback systems must guarantee absolute anonymity to respondents and confidentiality to employees regarding their feedback, or the process will fail. A bank instituted a 360° feedback process whereby the feedback providers confronted the employees directly in an open meeting. The results were highly inflated, and therefore useless, ratings for everyone and unhappy participants, who disliked the entire process.

360° assessment works only when respondent anonymity is assured. Many times people say, "We must trust one another around here and be honest with our feedback," or "We want people to be able to confront their rater directly, and get all the information out in the open." But this approach encourages people to give only positive information. People are not stupid: They will not give the difficult feedback if there is any chance the feedback can be traced to them. No amount of training changes this aspect of human behavior.

A public organization was confronted with a challenge in this area because one of its values was "open and honest communication." Initially the design team thought this value meant a commitment of openly confronting each employee with verbal feedback, but it still made parallel tests of public and anonymous feedback. It elected to use private feedback, concluding that the best way to receive honest feedback was to preserve the anonymity of the feedback provider. At the same time, it encouraged employees to have open communications with both their evaluation team members and other employees for specific feedback.

Similarly, rating procedures fail if the confidentiality of each employee's score is not protected. Such information has historically been confidential, known to only the employee, the employee's supervisor, and sometimes higher-level managers. The 360° feedback process must include safeguards that ensure the confidentiality of the employee's scores.

Competitive Procedures

Some organizations have introduced processes that compare one employee to another. Comparative formats force raters to make a judgment on which of two (or more) employees is the best on various criteria. The high rating of one employee thus comes at the expense of others. This competition creates unnecessary and unconstructive employee anxiety, leads to faulty results, and undermines cooperation and teamwork.

Rather than reflecting actual performance, a comparative system may be more a function of who is compared to whom. For example, analysis of multisource assessment at Gulf Oil verified that excellent performers in a high-performance group were seriously disadvantaged when the comparative system was used. The high performers were rated against other high performers, so some of them received a low rating overall. Analysis also indicated that employees in lower-level positions or those with less experience were seriously disadvantaged by direct comparisons with higher-level or more senior employees. Paired-comparison or other comparative processes significantly exaggerate hierarchy (level) bias.

Simple rating scale evaluations that do not compare people directly overcome many of the inherent problems associated with these comparative methods. In addition, nearly all the published research on multiple raters uses rating scales. The use of standard rating scales allows the assessment process to set the same performance standards for all employees.

Normative Comparisons

Some organizations create 360° feedback norms or organizational score averages for comparison. Each employee receives feedback showing not only a personal score for each item but also the group average. These comparisons can be devastating to employees.

A HIGH-TECH THINK TANK RETHINKS REPORTING NORMS

A high-tech aerospace think tank elected to use norms in reporting scores because the vendor-supplied multisource assessment process came prepackaged with "national norms." The organization had already used employee attitude surveys and its scientists and engineers were trained in using survey norms, so it thought the reporting system was a good idea. In fact, the use of norms was shattering to many of its employees, most of whom had been top students at the best schools and had been highly successful throughout their lives. Half of this population received scores below the average, and 80 percent received scores below the eightieth percentile. (A score below 80 percent is a failing grade in graduate school.)

Reporting the norms had these unforeseen, and unfortunate, consequences:

- Norms created a competitive focus as opposed to a cooperative and developmental emphasis.
- The employees focused on the scores of others rather than examining their own strengths and development areas.
- Employees correctly saw that the only way they could receive higher normed scores was to rate others lower.
- Employees became discouraged and anxious.

A group of scientists presented the argument to management that the norm comparisons were inappropriate, nonscientific, and indefensible with small samples. The organization listened to them and decided to use 360° feedback without norms.

Anyone considering using normative comparisons should review:

- Information acceptance by users with and without norms.
- The scientific rationale supporting the 360° feedback norms. Remember that these are not norms gathered for traditional survey information with large samples but for 360° feedback with small samples.
- The data used to create norms and how the organization would benefit from making comparisons (assuming such comparisons were valid) with other companies if using external norms.

Considerable literature supports the use of norms for traditional organizational surveys, but 360° feedback is distinctly different from these surveys. Many users expect to see norms in multisource assessment processes because many vendors provide them using the same methodology as norms for organizational climate and culture surveys. Before investing in the comparison to other organizations' 360° feedback scores, decide if such information adds value.

Misapplying 360° Feedback

The list of applications for which 360° feedback is not suitable is short yet important: selective targets, discipline and discharge, and reduction in force.

Selective Targets

One large communications organization instituted a multi-source system with the expressed purpose of targeting supervisors for elimination. Management wanted a flatter organization and created an upward review process to determine which supervisors should be retained. Not surprisingly, the project results were totally unreliable. So many direct reports gave erroneous feedback that the results could not be used for any purpose. Employees obviously felt the process was extremely unfair and resisted further attempts to use the process for any purpose.

Discipline and Discharge

Many professionals—military officers, CPAs, scientists, professors, pilots, lawyers, and doctors, among others—have used a process that appears similar to 360° feedback to make judgments regarding disciplinary and discharge actions. These peer review systems are well established, but the method and circumstances of use are substantially different from 360° feedback.

The peer review process uses a panel of assessors who are charged with making the difficult judgments regarding disciplinary or discharge action. As an expectation of service on the panel, assessors agree to provide their best judgments. In contrast, respondents in 360° feedback systems make no such agreement; their contribution is voluntary. They cannot be forced to make decisions if they do not want to because the resulting input would be spurious.

Reduction in Force

A large aerospace company implemented a multisource system in order to make retention decisions. The results were not sufficiently reliable to support retention decisions because employees were unwilling to participate, so there were many nonresponses; unwilling to injure another person's career, resulting in nearly uniformly positive responses; and willing to "game the system." Employees even came forward and told management exactly how they had colluded and manipulated the process to favor themselves (and injure others).

Ironically, respondents who respond honestly in these situations injure others because nearly everyone else responds only at the top of the scale. Experience shows people make this mistake only once. The next time they provide feedback, they tend to provide responses that are just as inflated as everyone else.

When a 360° feedback process has been in use for several years and people trust the results, then the 360° feedback measures are useful as one facet of the retention decision process. However, multisource systems are not likely to be the primary element of these types of decision processes because those who provide feedback do so voluntarily.

Learning From Others' Failures

Multisource systems present a number of unique opportunities for failure, as we have seen. These obstacles to 360° feedback implementation occur consistently and must be addressed. History indicates that many processes that fail lacked the administrative or organizational support to continue. Given all the potential challenges to 360° feedback systems, it becomes understandable why so few organizations have successfully implemented the process or even tried. Fortunately, these obstacles may be overcome by anticipating and addressing them effectively in the process design stages.

When organizations resolve the concerns and adopt 360° feedback, the appraisal system becomes more accurate and trustworthy. Effective processes require respondent anonymity, ratee confidentiality, modest administrative overhead, internal commitment, and top management support. In order to achieve the goal of fairness and accuracy in performance measurement procedures, these commitments are critically important. Managers and employees can then enjoy substantial benefits, including the knowledge that the most deserving performers will be identified accurately and rewarded appropriately.

8

Addressing Criticisms of 360° Feedback

In spite of every sage whom Greece can show,
Unerring wisdom never dwelt below;
Folly in all of every age we see,
The only difference lies in the degree.
                    —Satire, Greek philosopher

Once authority is out of the bottle and has seeped
throughout the organization, people do not want to return
to the old days of drops of authority from a single, tightly
regulated spigot.
            —Peter B. Vail, author of *Continuous Whitewater*

Most design teams find themselves confronting criticisms when implementing the 360° feedback process. Employees and managers alike may express predictable concerns, and nearly every organization has naysayers who openly criticize any new process. Organizations must quickly and thoughtfully address these criticisms to prevent the entire project from failing.

Anticipating Common Concerns

Predictable concerns are worded in many different ways, yet each really asks the same question: "So what? What is the value added by this process?" To the following common questions and criticisms, we provide effective responses.

- *How do you know that 360° feedback improves productivity?* Good managers make data-driven decisions. They want hard data to support their decision to move from single to multirater assessments. Some managers are moved by compelling empirical research supporting the accuracy and validity of multiple- as opposed to single-rater systems.

One of the best ways to assess whether 360° feedback systems influence individual, team, or organization productivity is to ask participants. Postproject assessments from surveys, focus groups, and interviews usually show clear evidence that most users believe feedback from multiple credible sources improves productivity. Findings from the evaluation stage can help an organization demonstrate increased productivity due to 360° feedback.

Nearly any member of an organization that uses 360° systems can point to individuals whose behavior has changed substantially as a result; instead of simply trying to please their boss, they realized the importance of saving their internal and external customers too.

Pat Riley, the professional basketball coach, notes that professional athletes are not highly motivated by the coach alone. In fact, they are tough to motivate because they are paid so handsomely. But when they receive feedback from their teammates on their "hustle factor"—their effort demonstrated on the basketball floor—they are motivated to hustle, recovering loose balls and playing aggressive defense. Pat Riley says that structured feedback on the hustle factor from teammates translates to an additional 3 or 4 points a game. For many people, peer pressure is a powerful motivator.

- *360° feedback will reward the "nice" people who don't do any work.* Some people argue that those who do things well may not be getting the right things done, but surveys of supervisors using 360° feedback for evaluation report strong correspondence between competencies and results. Employees who do not accomplish their action plans and work responsibilities seldom fool anyone.

ARIZONA PUBLIC SERVICE CONFIRMS THE ACCURACY OF MULTISOURCE ASSESSMENT

At Arizona Public Service, forty-four word processors were evaluated on their behavioral competencies using multisource assessment. Unknown to the coworkers who provided the responses, management conducted a separate evaluation using the number of keystrokes to measure quantity and quality of work. The result was a strong agreement between the two sets of data; the correlation between the outcome measure that quantified word processor productivity and the behavioral scores was 0.87. Thus, the 360° feedback process identified those who were the most productive word processors.

One interesting piece of information emerged from this study: One word processor was much more productive than others in terms of the online measure of keystroke quantity and quality, but she was so disruptive when she interacted with others that she received low behavior feedback scores from her coworkers. Employees tend to favor both high productivity and strong team member skills.

• *Some people will receive behavior feedback and still not change.* True, some people ignore advice from everyone—their doctor, their friends, their spouse. And certainly some people do not change their behaviors when they receive feedback from only the immediate supervisor. However, most people find the combined feedback from their supervisor and coworkers highly motivating. Most people are sensitive to and respond to constructive behavior feedback, and most also seek the esteem of their teammates.

• *Why bother with a 360° feedback process if there is little difference from supervisor-only ratings?* Different organizations start at different points. Many organizations' single-source assessment processes provide ratings that do not show a distinct difference between high, medium, or low performance. Also, traditional supervisor-only appraisals too often reward the wrong behaviors and leadership styles. For most feedback receivers, capturing information from a number of coworkers is radically different from receiving that of the supervisor alone.

The 360° feedback process, unlike single-source evaluations, is more fair when further analysis is done on diversity measures, such as age, gender, and ethnicity. In addition, 360° feedback processes have been able to identify other valuable performers: quiet contributors, sometimes called "woodwork," who do not blow their own horn; nonpoliticals, who do not engage in office or company politics; creative champions, who, while not being creative themselves, engender creativity in others; and internal trainers, who develop others at the expense of their own output.

• *It costs too much.* Training expenses, likely to be $50 to $150 per person for the important training, are necessary with the implementation of any culture change or performance measurement process. Experience shows that the typical investment in 360° feedback software ranges from $70 to $200, depending on the sophistication of the technology and the number of users. When amortized over four years, assuming use twice a year, the investment amounts to between $5 and $20 per use. As technology improves and networked-based electronic assessment replaces paper surveys, direct costs per use will become minimal.

Managers often contrast this cost with the current supervisor-only appraisal process that *seems* to cost nothing. However, when indirect costs are assessed, such as supervisory and administrative time, single-source systems become expensive in comparison. Westinghouse, for example, found that supervisors spent about 4 hours on each direct report. Contrasted with the 15 to 30 minutes they reported with the 360° feedback process, they preferred the 360° feedback.

Opportunity costs may also be ignored. What is the opportunity cost of not having accurate and motivating performance feedback? What costs are added when an organization must take legal action because the single-source appraisal process is not fair? Most people do not think in terms of opportunities that are lost by not using 360° feedback, but an employee focus group can create a long list very quickly.

• *The process takes too much time.* Organizations must provide employees time to participate in training and time for completing surveys. Typically, pre- and postfeedback training, necessary only for the first cycle, takes 3 to 6 hours, and the time to respond to surveys, assuming an average of seven surveys, is 1½ hours. The process design team should make every effort to minimize the time investment so that the organizational cost of the time invested exceeds the value of the performance measures.

Some employees worry that they will be asked to complete too many surveys and therefore will spend all their time responding to surveys. Typically, however, less than 2 percent of all nonsupervisory respondents are asked to be on more than fifteen teams. Some supervisors do complete more evaluations, as would be expected in that responsibility.

The new assessment models are minimizing respondent time requirements. For example, the rating for supervisors who have a large span of control, such as more than forty direct reports, can be combined. Or these supervisors may elect not to provide feedback for some people with whom they do not work closely.

Similarly, when twenty or more employees report to a supervisor, it may make sense to sample them rather than have everyone provide feedback. At one Allied Signal division, eight direct reports are chosen at random from the pool of all people reporting to a manager. Anyone who is not selected yet wants to provide feedback to the manager may do so. This voluntary feedback is combined with the eight respondents selected at random.

Research shows that those who are selected to serve on many evaluation teams often are chosen because they are accurate with their feedback. They may have job responsibilities requiring interaction with the subject and may be able to provide valuable insight. Conversely, respondents who are chosen by a very few people are not as accurate as a group with their responses as those selected by many other people. Research on respondent selection suggests that people seem not to know who responds leniently or harshly but they do know who is likely to be inaccurate. These inaccurate people are largely left out of the selection process when employees are allowed to select their own evaluation team. Hence, this assessment model avoids a potential source of substantial distortion.

A courtesy guideline accommodates user concerns about one person's being selected by too many others to provide feedback:

> "As a courtesy, please ask the people whom you have selected for your evaluation if they feel comfortable providing feedback to you. Someone who already has been asked by too many others or a person does not feel he or she has enough contact may decline."

This courtesy guideline, a "high-touch" solution, works better than a "high-tech" solution where a computer program limits the number of times a person can be asked to provide feedback.

MCDONNELL-DOUGLAS USES A SUPERVISOR'S SAMPLE FROM A SET OF DIRECT REPORTS

At McDonnell-Douglas, as in many other organizations, the spans of control increased from one-to-eight to one-to-twelve, -twenty-five, or -thirty-five—and sometimes even higher. In order to keep response time reasonable, the employee design team looked into methods to minimizing the time spent in the 360° feedback process. In the experiment they set up, each manager selected a "first five" evaluation team of direct reports. Each manager was assessed by the entire group of direct reports, which included the manager's previously designated "first five," and received two behavior feedback profiles: one with scores of the "first five" and the other with scores of all the direct reports.

The research results were conclusive: The two sets of profiles were almost identical, and the consistency between these two groups' scores was very high with a correlation coefficient of 0.91. The experiment showed that a sample of direct reports would provide nearly the same behavior feedback as a census, which resulted in an interesting policy decision: The organization would now randomly sample the direct report set for eight respondents during each 360° feedback cycle. In addition, any direct report who did not get selected yet wanted to provide feedback to the supervisor could voluntarily join the evaluation team. Every two years, all direct reports provide feedback.

• All other arguments notwithstanding, if an organization cannot sufficiently minimize respondent and administrative time, 360° feedback projects will not survive. A response time formula can help determine survey response time:

1. Time several typical respondents to estimate how long it takes to complete the survey.
2. Multiply the response time by the number of members on the average evaluation team. The result is the response time per employee.
3. Multiply this number by the number of people receiving feedback in the project.
4. Convert the response hours to workdays by dividing by 8.

Figure 8-1. Respondent time investment table for Evaluation Team Size = 12 in Work Days (8 hours)

Survey Response Time (hours) for 1 respondent	Number of Participants						
	50	100	200	400	800	1600	3200
.125 (10 min.)	9.4	18.8	37.5	75	150	300	600
.25 (15 min.)	18.8	37.5	75	150	300	600	1200
.5 (30 min.)	37.5	75	150	300	600	1200	2400
1 (60 min.)	75	150	300	600	1200	2400	4800

Notes: 1. Respondents typically respond at the rate of three items a minute. Hence, a 90 item survey requires about 30 minutes for response.
           2. Half the time requirements for evaluation teams size = 6.

The result is the *total time investment*. For example, a survey that takes approximately 15 minutes to complete, has an evaluation team size of 12, with 200 participants results in a total time cost to the organization of 600 hours or 75 workdays.

An estimate of the time investment for various length surveys and numbers of participants can be made quickly from Figure 8-1. For example, a 30-minute survey used by 100 people who received feedback would cost the organization about 75 workdays in respondent time. Here is the calculation:

0.5 hour per respondent × 12 respondents for each feedback receiver =
6 hours per participant
6 hours per participant × 100 participants = 600 hours
600 hours / 8 hours perwork day = 75 workdays

Modest changes in process parameters have a substantial impact on the total time investments. For example, reducing evaluation teams from twelve to six members cuts the time investment in half, to 37.5 workdays. If the survey is also shortened so response time drops from 30 to 15 minutes, total response time is cut in half again, to 18.8 workdays.

These time investment illustrations indicate why it is important to keep surveys short and evaluation teams reasonably small. Additionally, even modest changes in survey response time or the size of the average evaluation team can produce dramatic changes in the total organizational time investment.

Following the recommendations below will enable an organization to use 360° feedback in a manner that reduces supervisory time and requires a similar total organization time investment:

1. Communicate employee actions and competencies (questions) in advance. This reduces the time necessary when employees provide feedback.
2. Train respondents before they provide feedback.
3. Create respondent instructions that encourage fast responses.
4. Keep surveys short.
5. Use a short format for constructs or questions. This can halve response speed. (A short format uses a short phrase rather than a full sentence for each question.)
6. Minimize the amount of time in which respondents can complete their surveys. Give respondents a two-week window to respond rather than a month.
7. Capture responses electronically using computer disks, e-mail, or a network.
8. Automate the input, administration, and scoring process.
9. Measure time investments for training, responding, and administration; then improve the process to minimize all time costs.

Ask participants for their ideas on process improvements:

— How long did it take to provide feedback for one person?
— Did this response time feel too short, about right, or too long?
— In your opinion, how long should the process of providing feedback take?
— Do you have any ideas for improving the process of providing feedback?

Management and employees always ask how much time the 360° feedback process requires. The only way to provide an accurate answer is to measure relevant aspects of the 360° feedback process, including response time for feedback providers and administrative time for process administrators.

WESTINGHOUSE MEASURES TIME COSTS
FOR SINGLE- AND MULTIPLE-SOURCE SYSTEMS

Westinghouse found that the 360° feedback process required less evaluation time than the traditional supervisor-only appraisal for supervisors but more time for employees. Net to the organization, though, the time investment turned out to be about the same. More important, the 360° feedback process provided substantial improvements in user satisfaction with feedback, teamwork, and productivity.

An important consideration in this research was supervisory time because supervisors had numerous responsibilities. Ninety-four percent of the supervisors supported the multisource process, which substantially reduced the amount of time required of them to conduct performance reviews. The estimates at Westinghouse for supervisors were as follows:

	Single Source	*360° Feedback*
Time required to evaluate one person	2–4 hours	15–30 minutes

The time savings by supervisors was offset by employees' providing feedback. Nonsupervisory employees reported the 360° feedback took them 10 to 15 minutes per survey. Since each employee received feedback from four or five others besides the supervisor, response time for each participant was less than 90 minutes. Using the survey estimates, total assessment time investment per person was:

	Supervisor	+ Employees	= Total Time
Supervisor only	2–4 hours	0	= 2–4 hours
360° feedback	30 minutes	15 minutes × 5=	about 2 hours

Most supervisors who do a good job of documenting the traditional appraisal process report they invest 2 or more hours in their task for each assessment. When the 360° feedback process uses a short survey and reasonably small evaluation teams, the time investments for the traditional and the new process will be similar.

• *No one is available to operate the 360° feedback process.* Organizations have reduced employee populations, which often means no one is available to coordinate the tasks associated with creating, sending, receiving, scoring and processing, and returning behavior feedback results. Paper-based 360° feedback systems need three or four people per 1,000 users. Automated processes reduce this requirement to one person per 2,000 who can work during the six to eight weeks when the formal process occurs. If an organization does not want to invest in internal processes, it can outsource its process and substantially reduce assessment time.

• *The 360° feedback process creates so much information that it overwhelms participants.* Organizations must remember to keep surveys short, simple, and clear. A feedback process that is complicated to respondents creates errors through respondent fatigue and possible misunderstanding of questions. Similarly, the behavior feedback reports should be short, simple, and clear so employees understand what the information means and can act effectively on it.

• *The process is a passing fad.* True, 360° feedback systems are becoming a fad in the sense that organizational trials of the new model are accelerating. Whether they continue depends on the productivity impact of the feedback. If the 360° feedback process does indeed improve productivity and create better evaluations for managers and employees, the fad will grow into a trend and even become the standard operating procedure for assessing and developing people at work.

• *The 360° feedback process creates a beauty contest, where popularity or sociability is more important than performance.* No other argument has been presented more often than the concern about popularity bias. Those who present this argument seem to forget that single-source assessments have been consistently criticized as a political or popularity contest with the boss.

At Disney, the issue of popularity was addressed scientifically by studying participant response patterns to job-related criteria and to popularity. The 360° feedback research study for 122 employees in the merchandising division of Disney's EPCOT used both job-related competencies and a "hold-out" construct, popularity (that is, popularity was held out of the behavior feedback reports). The researchers did not want to give people feedback that told them they were unpopular.

The study found that popularity was only modestly associated with performance, with a correlation coefficient of 0.34. However, all other job-related criteria (such as "communications skills") had more than double that of the 0.34 correlation with overall performance.

In the Disney project, one of the most popular individuals was last in overall performance. He was known to coworkers as "Mr. Sports" because every Thursday and Friday, he walked the halls predicting sports scores, and every Monday and Tuesday, he reported the weekend scores. Conversely, there were some high performers who were not rated very popularly. Hence, the multiple respondents do assess job performance or behaviorally demonstrated competencies with only a modest influence by popularity.

• *Different respondents are going to use the scale differently. One evaluation panel should rate all people in each area.* Evaluation panels, with one evaluation team for everyone, are used by some organizations and in special circumstances, such as extremely technical jobs where expert knowledge is needed to evaluate competencies. Evaluation committees are also common in small groups like departments at universities.

A panel evaluation assumes that each of the panel members has sufficient contact with each of the employees to provide a valid evaluation. Unfortunately, most people interact with only four to nine coworkers who have sufficient contact to provide high-quality behavior feedback.

The theoretical gain from a standard evaluation panel, in terms of response consistency, is completely undermined by the problem that many panel members lack sufficient knowledge of performance for some people they are asked to assess. Since the 360° feedback process is based on tapping the knowledge network, distributed evaluation teams, where each assessee's evaluation team is unique, create more accurate information.

Statistical analysis indicates that distributed evaluation teams are quite consistent with one another. People who are responding honestly tend to use approximately the same metric standard in their responses. An easy test of this concept is the *two-team test*, which allows employees to select two different evaluation teams. The idea behind the two-team test is to examine the reliability of the 360° feedback process when the subject, the assessee, selects two different evaluation teams. Research at Gulf Oil, Arizona State University, Westinghouse, Dow Chemical, and Bell of Pennsylvania has shown that, assuming similar degree of contact and perspectives are represented on each evaluation team, nine times out of ten the dual evaluation teams provide a composite result that is within 7 percent of one another. Hence, not only do distributed evaluation teams work; they work exceedingly well in providing a reliable performance measure.

A useful safeguard that addresses the possible differences among distributed evaluation teams is called the *team rigor index;* it sums each respondent's average use of the rating scale across all their assessments. If two respondents provide feedback and one averages 7.9 and the other 6.2 on a 10-point rating scale, the 6.2 is more rigorous because the average rating is lower on the scale. More rigorous ratings are tougher. Using each respondent's average rigor score, a team rigor index can be created for every evaluation team. The average rigor of every evaluation team can be compared with all others. This safeguard shows that distributed evaluation teams are consistent in their relative degree of evaluation rigor. Such a safeguard also answers the potentially difficult question: "Was my evaluation team by chance tougher than others?"

• *People will select their friends rather than the people they should for their evaluation teams.* Another common critique occurs regarding the issue of potential friendship bias. Although the research suggests that friendship has little influence in confidential responses, people often question the research.

Another approach is to ask the question, "Doesn't everyone have the same opportunity to select friends?" The answer is yes. In measurement terms, if everyone selects friends, everyone has the same advantage. The anticipated influence of friendship is inflated responses, which would theoretically skew the entire performance distribution toward the high end. Fortunately, inflated responses and the skew of the performance distribution are simple to measure as a process safeguard.

Possibly the best response to those who are adamant about friendship bias is the two-team test. The two-team test, where participants select one team of friends and one team of nonfriends, shows the composite scores of the two teams are within 7 percent of one another over 90 percent of the time.

Figure 8-2. The two-team test at Disney: Snow Whites (friends) versus Grumpies (nonfriends).

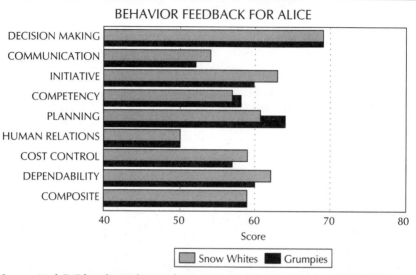

BEHAVIOR FEEDBACK FOR ALICE

DECISION MAKING
COMMUNICATION
INITIATIVE
COMPETENCY
PLANNING
HUMAN RELATIONS
COST CONTROL
DEPENDABILITY
COMPOSITE

40　　　50　　　60　　　70　　　80

Score

Snow Whites　Grumpies

Source: Mark R. Edwards, "Making Performance Appraisals Meaningful and Fair," *Business* (July–September 1989).

When presented the opportunity to provide anonymous feedback, people are candid regardless of friendships.

DISNEY'S "ALICE" GETS SIMILAR SCORES FROM "SNOW WHITES" AND "GRUMPIES"

The issue of evaluation team selection at Disney led to a test of evaluation team consistency in 1981. After an initial pilot project, some people were concerned that friendship bias would enter respondent selection. Participants who were skeptical about the 360° feedback process were allowed to select two separate evaluation teams. They were asked to select teams with members who had similar perspectives: colleagues, direct reports, or mixed. Figure 8-2 shows that even when "Alice" selected her "Snow Whites" on one team and put a set of "Grumpies" on the other, the results were nearly identical. Of twenty-two people who selected dual evaluation teams in this project, only two received team behavior profiles that differed more than 7 percent on the composite score.

Selected participants at Humana Hospital, Arizona State University, Westinghouse, du Pont and Chicago Osteopathic Health Services even selected three different evaluation teams. All of these triads of evaluation teams were consistent with one another. Usually each of the three teams agrees on the shape of the profile, indicating the subject's highest and lowest competencies.

Many of the criticisms presented about 360° feedback turn out to be minimal. Although each organization has a unique perspective based on its own priorities, there also are similarities among the considerations raised. If the organization does not respond to employee criticisms through the communications activities, they create significant employee resistance that is extremely difficult to overcome.

These additional concerns, shown in Figure 8-3, are paired with reasonable responses based on field experience in many different organizational environments. Most of the concerns derive from fear. 360° feedback changes the rules, for both the organization and its employees. It is revolutionary to many who have attained their organizational positions following the old rules. The important issue about concerns is to anticipate and understand what they will be and then systematically respond to them.

Appeals Procedures

One important way an organization can address process concerns is by creating an appeals procedure. Employees want to know that an appeals process is in place, and they want to know how it works with the 360° feedback system.

The appeals procedure offers a valuable step in process validation. A variety of these processes have been developed; Arizona State University's is simple and fair and has served a wide variety of organizations since it was designed in 1984.

ARIZONA STATE UNIVERSITY DESIGNS 360° FEEDBACK
APPEALS PROCEDURE

The design team created an appeals procedure in support of the 360° feedback process. Anyone who wished to appeal had a simple task:

(text continues page 180)

Figure 8-3. Effective responses to employee concerns.

Objection	Effective Response
Fear of the process	Pilot the process. Experience overcomes most fears.
Understanding the process	Use lateral learning. Benchmark best practices by learning from the experience of successful others.
It is too different; it is upside down from current practice	Find aligned organization initiatives like empowered leaders, customer service, quality improvement processes, teams, and reengineering actions.
It will take too long for supervisors	Find out how much time supervisors spend on the current system. Pilot a process and ask supervisors the same question. Supervisors often report that 360° feedback reduces evaluation time for them by 50 percent or more, and it automates otherwise tedious documentation.
It will take too long for employees	Ask employees how much time they are willing to invest in providing others high-quality feedback in order to receive high-quality feedback themselves. Design the system to stay within these time parameters.
Many employees will not respond	Pilot the process. Experience overcomes this fear. Nonrespondents should be below 15 percent.
It will cost too much	Figure out an estimated budget and begin to sell it. Calculations may start with per-person, one-time investments around $100 for training and $50 for technology.
Supervisors will not support it; it breaks the unity-of-command concept	Pilot the process. Experience shows supervisors embrace multisource assessment even faster than independent contributors do.
Supervisors will abdicate their responsibility for evaluation	Include specific questions in the survey regarding supervisors' providing honest feedback and supporting employee development. Accountability motivates behavior change.

(continues)

Figure 8-3. (*continued*)

Objection	Effective Response
Users will not accept anonymity	Ask them. Surveys show that nineteen of twenty users prefer anonymity.
We will not be able to support respondent anonymity legally	If user surveys show high preference for anonymity and process communications ensure respondents anonymity, it is difficult to create a legal argument to undermine the contract of anonymity.
Senior management may not find time to respond	Use the built-in solution to senior respondent deliquency: show the "S" for the supervisory rating on the reports. Accountability motivates behavior.
Senior management will not support the process	Pilot the process. Experience shows senior management are among the strongest process supporters, if they receive process training.
Supervisors (or others) will retaliate	Address this serious threat with a dual solution: Use an instrument construct such as "treats people fairly" and include safeguards that ensure respondent anonymity.
If the responses are so fast, they cannot be accurate	Ask the following question: "What does the research show about test taking? Who make higher scores: those who answer quickly or those who spend a long time pondering each answer?"
People will not be able to find enough good evaluators	Pilot the process. Experience shows nearly everyone can find a handful of others who can provide high-quality feedback. Those who cannot may be able to find ways to give more exposure to others.
Users will want narrative feedback	Yes. Research shows the narratives are the most valuable feedback to many participants. Remember that an automated feedback system will multiply the number of narrative comments provided.

Objection	Effective Response
Some people will try to game the system to their favor	Yes. Consequently safeguards such as intelligent scoring and reporting are necessary to moderate games players. Unless this concern is addressed, it will be fatal to the process since it will destroy the integrity of the assessment information.
Union people will not provide feedback	Pilot the process. Ask for feedback on a voluntary basis from union members. Experience has been positive with union willingness to provide feedback, especially for supervisors or leaders.
The union will not support participation.	Allow union representatives to participate in the process design and to view and examine the process evaluation. Some union groups have seen the process work in the organization and then ask to participate as feedback providers and receivers.
Friendship will bias the results	Read the empirical research on friendship bias. It shows that friends usually provide honest feedback. In some cases, friends may be more rigorous than others, due possibly to higher expectations.
Competition will bias the results	While there is little published research on competition bias, our research shows most respondents are honest. Multisource assessment systems without safeguards to moderate competition bias will predictably report substantial distortion where it occurs.
Respondents will "gang up" on others, especially to a supervisor	Pilot the process. Experience overcomes most fears, including this one. Multisource assessment systems are very robust when the sources of obvious distortion are removed.
Competition will destroy teamwork	Pilot the process. Users consistently report these processes are strong supporters of teamwork. They do, however, very clearly identify if a team member is not supporting the team.

select a second evaluation team. But no one appealed their 360° feedback results in several years of tracking the process at the University. Rather, many elected to test it at the front end of the process. More than sixty faculty and about two dozen administrators selected two separate evaluation teams to explore the reliability of process results.

Universities are unusual in that most departments are relatively small and most faculty know the other department members fairly well. Therefore, many faculty could find two teams of five to seven members who knew them well enough to provide assessments. Some participants tried to stack the deck with one team composed of friends and the other made up of nonfriends. The consistent result from most of these dual evaluation teams was a composite score within 7 percent between the friends and nonfriends teams.

Several participants noted that even though the results from the two evaluations were very similar, their "friends" were more rigorous in their assessments than were "nonfriends." Evidently friends may have higher expectations. (Or could it be that some people just don't know who their friends are?)

Responding Effectively to Gain Support

360° feedback provides a valuable source of developmental and appraisal information for employees, but the substantial benefits are available only if the predictable objections are anticipated and addressed. Project administrators and the design team should anticipate a blizzard of employee concerns and criticisms and be ready to respond to them effectively.

9

The Promise of 360° Feedback

There is almost no troubled situation that cannot be
improved by rearranging it to distribute power more
equally.

—Virginia Satir, American author

There are and can be only two ways of searching into
and discovering truth. The one flies from the senses and
particulars to the most general axioms . . . this way is
now in fashion. The other derives axioms from the senses
and particulars, rising by a gradual and unbroken ascent,
so that it arrives at the most general axioms last of all.
This is the true way, but as yet untried.

—Sir Francis Bacon

The promise of 360° feedback becomes visible from extraordinary
process results: improved employee satisfaction with the work environment, significant behavior changes aligned with organization
values and objectives, and better individual and team performance
that goes beyond employees to external customers, who buy goods
and services.

Seldom has a new tool captured the imagination of both academicians and industry leaders as quickly as 360° feedback. Organizations are learning what top academicians have been saying
for many years: Feedback from multiple sources makes sense and
can improve productivity.

Translating the promise of multisource assessment processes
into sustainable systems is now the challenge. The process must

do what it is supposed to do: create fair and accurate performance measures that motivate employees and strengthen development. If it does not, users will dismiss the 360° feedback initiatives as a passing fad.

The Impacts of 360° Feedback

The 360° feedback process has a dramatic impact on employees, managers, teams, and organizations. As evidence to show the process really works, many organizations have developed measures associated with total quality management initiatives from existing employee survey data. Other baseline measures may be available too—for example:

- customer satisfaction
- leadership
- supervision
- work
- diversity
- performance feedback
- product/service quality
- career development
- performance appraisal

- pay
- promotion
- job assignments
- employee satisfaction
- morale
- turnover
- attendance
- safety
- other rewards

After implementing a 360° feedback process, project administrators can compare these data taken under the traditional model with those from the new feedback process.

Evaluation Preferences

Research from dozens of organizations shows that most employees prefer to receive feedback from more people than just their supervisor. For example, results from a pilot postproject evaluation at Coca-Cola USA Fountain, Figure 9-1, showed only 3.9 percent felt feedback should come only from the supervisor while 94.8 percent felt feedback should come from both supervisor and coworkers.

Figure 9-1. Results of survey of Coca-Cola Fountain employees on who should provide feedback.

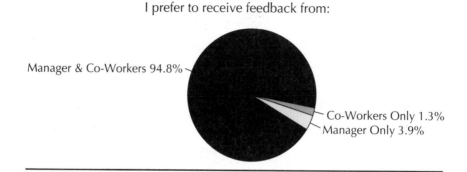

I prefer to receive feedback from:

Manager & Co-Workers 94.8%

Co-Workers Only 1.3%
Manager Only 3.9%

User Satisfaction

The most relevant measure of process effectiveness comes from user satisfaction surveys of the performance appraisal process. The best way to determine the validity of a 360° feedback process is to ask users whether the process met project objectives, such as fairness, accuracy, or simplicity. User satisfaction surveys provide a strong indication of how various stakeholders feel about the process and whether they support its continued use.

These project assessments provide clear information about critical success factors. Houlihan's postpilot project evaluation, shown in Figure 9-2, illustrates typical responses for the restaurant operations. Nearly all participants felt the 360° feedback process provides useful results. About 95 percent felt the process was motivational and simple to use. The least support occurred for whether 360° feedback was a complete assessment, whether the subject should select the evaluation team, and whether training time was well spent. The posttest evaluation results identify areas for training and process changes.

User support for important process elements, such as respondent anonymity, fairness, and time efficiency, is valuable to process validation. Comments from the surveys provide rich narrative information for future process improvements. Similarly, focus

Figure 9-2. Houlihan's post pilot project user satisfaction survey results.

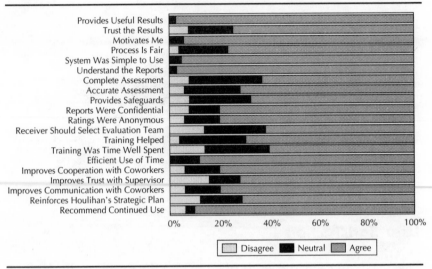

groups, interviews, and staff meetings reinforce the validity of the 360° feedback process to various stakeholders.

Pre- and Postproject Assessments

Project surveys should also assess whether users prefer the new multisource process or the old single-source, supervisor-only system. These surveys usually reveal substantial preference for the new 360° feedback process.

These assessments may be tailored to measure specific participant reactions based on the design team objectives.

Perceived Fairness

A study that looked at how users in sixteen companies viewed process fairness and value-added found that about 80 percent of the respondents believed the process was fair (Figure 9-3). The user sample was a diverse group: Arizona State University, Arizona Public Service, Mesa Schools, Pima County, Kino Hospital, Salt River Project, G. A. Technologies, Arizona Commerce Bank,

Figure 9-3. Perceptions of process fairness across sixteen organizations.

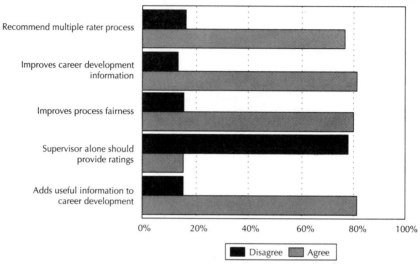

Notes: Projects ranged from 44 to 1,272 participants.
Scores do not add to 100 because neutrals are not shown.

Source: Mark R. Edwards, "Sustaining Culture Change with Multiple Rater Systems for Career Development and Performance Appraisal Systems," in *The Corporate Culture Sourcebook* (Boston: HRD Press, 1990).

Bell of Pennsylvania, Current, Inc., Westinghouse, Esso Resources, Gulf Oil, Fidelity Bank, US West, and Disney. These data are consistent with other information. User satisfaction rates for traditional single-source appraisals, based on our own 1994 survey across eighty-two organizations, showed satisfaction levels between 5 and 35 percent, with a mean of 26 percent. Much of the dissatisfaction stemmed from employees' perceptions that the process was unfair. In organizations that introduced 360° feedback, the difference between perceived fairness for traditional, single-source performance measures and 360° feedback increased over 50 percent.

Another way of looking at these results suggests that a change of the assessment model, from single to multiple source, yields an increase in perceived fairness from unsatisfied to satisfied for half the employee population. These results, which have been repli-

Figure 9-4.   Distribution of sources using the single-source model.

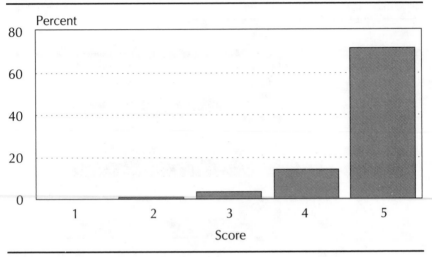

cated many times, argue that the 360° feedback model produces performance measures that users perceived as fair.

A substantial limitation to this research is that only a few of the reported assessments occurred for organizations with more than five years of 360° feedback experience. Since 360° feedback is relatively new to most organizations, this data may be partially explained by a Hawthorne effect (whereby any change creates a temporary improvement). However, preliminary data from research indicates that user assessment of long-term 360° feedback systems remains stable at over 80 percent support.

Distribution Measures

An examination of pre- and postproject assessment score distributions—that is, the spread of scores—usually shows substantial differences between a single-source and a multisource assessment process. Most organizations find that the traditional single-source assessment information results in a performance distribution where all the performance measures are clumped at the top of the scale range, as illustrated in Figure 9-4. In contrast, 360° feedback systems, with trained users, scoring safeguards, and a 10-point scale, create substantially more distinction across the distribution,

Figure 9-5. Distribution of scores using the 360° feedback model.

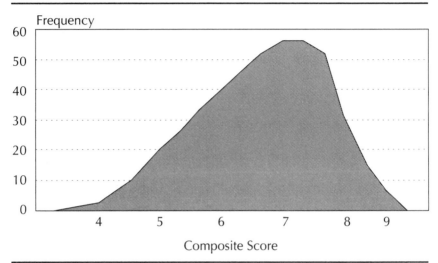

as shown in Figure 9-5. This wider distribution approximates the average distribution across thirty-five multisource projects representing over 48,000 participants who received feedback. The wider distribution means that differential rewards may be made with more equity and credibility to users.

Analysis across these thirty-five projects indicates the 360° feedback widens the score distribution compared to the traditional supervisor-only appraisal systems by about four times. The primary variables attributed to this wider spread of scores are as follows:

- Work associates do not share the same self-serving biases as supervisors to inflate performance ratings.
- Most respondents respond honestly and without substantial inflation when ensured of absolute anonymity (the feedback receiver never knows how any one person rated).
- Most respondents who are trained in the process of providing feedback respond honestly.
- Process safeguards, such as intelligent scoring, remove obviously invalid respondents.

- A 10-point response scale allows respondents to provide more distinction among scale points than with a 5-point scale.

The implications of the wider spread of performance measures are substantial. In an era when many organizations are fighting entitlements, a wider and more valid spread of performance scores makes differential recognition and reward easier and more credible. Nearly any traditional recognition and rewards policy will work better with improved validity of performance measures. The wider distribution of performance scores creates more sensitive measures that can reveal relatively small differences in behavior.

Measures of Behavior Change

Organizations are searching for meaningful methods to measure the effectiveness of training. Unfortunately, single-source appraisal measures usually are so inflated that attempting to correlate the data with training programs typically produces no solid information. Since nearly everyone receives high performance measures, those who change behaviors and those who do not look alike in a quantitative analysis.

Since 360° feedback systems are sensitive to modest changes of behavior, they are more likely to show any impact of training and development processes. Figure 9-6 shows the impacts of training effectiveness. A manufacturing firm tracked people who received training in the areas of customer service and team building. The three time periods of assessment show improvement in most behaviors. Although this research would be stronger with a control group, the results nevertheless show positive behavior changes associated with the targeted training.

Identifying Substance Abusers

A coincidental finding associated with the 360° feedback model has been the identification of substance abusers. Single-source measures are unlikely to identify substance abuse problems because supervisors shy away from confronting employees with be-

Figure 9-6. Measuring training effectiveness.

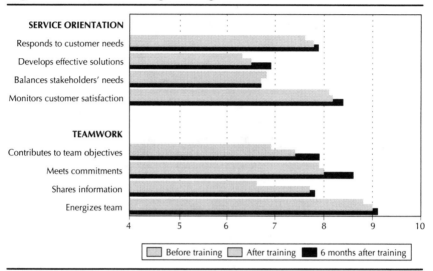

havior problems. Substance abusers often play cat and mouse with their supervisor, shielding the supervisor from the behavioral impacts of substance abuse. Imagine how difficult it is for a supervisor to confront a substance abuser without corroborating evidence from others. Coworkers, on the other hand, are usually able and willing to provide highly consistent feedback on a substance abuser's behaviors. They may also document examples of inappropriate or unsafe behavior.

The identification of suspected substance abuse has occurred in numerous 360° feedback projects, usually from one of three conditions:

1. The behavior profile, while generally strong, shows one or more very low items, such as dependability (Figure 9-7). The condition may be called the *amputated profile* because one key competency, often associated with dependability, seems to have an amputated score.
2. A behavior profile that represents a sequence of multiple time periods shows a significant degradation of performance scores over two or more performance periods.

Figure 9-7. Behavior profile identifying possible substance abuse.

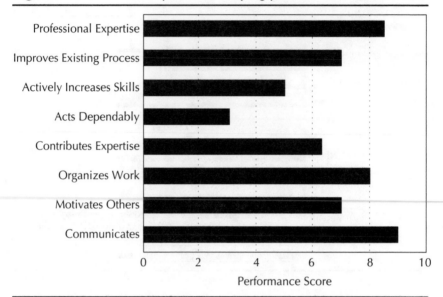

3. The behavior profile shows a substantial gap between the supervisor's rating and that of others. Often the supervisor is the last to know about a substance abuse problem.

Such flags do not conclusively identify substance abuse, but they clearly indicate the need for some intervention, possibly training related, but more appropriately a referral to an employee assistance program. Early identification of serious problems can save not only careers but also lives.

Productivity Measures

Organizations always have grappled with how to measure productivity. 360° feedback projects have been able to define and enhance organizational productivity. The following direct and indirect productivity indicators may be linked to 360° feedback processes:

- Increases in product quantity or quality
- Reduction in errors, returns, or defects

Figure 9-8. Research productivity impacts at a university: single-source versus multisource assessment.

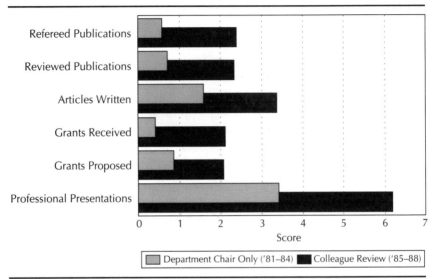

- Decreases in raw material, scrap, or other costs
- Improvements in safety, such as a decrease in accidents

The year after Westinghouse's Steam Turbine Generator Division in Orlando, Florida, implemented a 360° feedback project for performance management, the human resources manager, George Dann, announced a 28 percent productivity increase for the plant. Although a number of factors interacted to create the productivity increase, the change brought about by the multisource assessment process was the major organization development intervention.

A study of university professors in one department at Arizona State University demonstrates a form of productivity measurement. Figure 9-8 shows the baseline measures for research productivity over a five-year period when the professors were evaluated singularly by the department chair. During a four-year period when professors were evaluated by colleagues and the department chair, research productivity increased substantially. During the period of multisource use, merit money either was insignificant or absent at the university. Hence, money impacts did not explain the changes in research productivity.

A graduate student reported a plausible explanation based on his interviews and focus groups with faculty. He quoted a faculty member:

"I felt no compelling reason to listen to the advice on performance feedback I received when my department chair reviewed my activities. I had neither research publications nor any grant proposals. However, when I knew my peers were to look at my research record, I wanted to avoid embarrassment in front of my professional colleagues. This was my first publication in fifteen years."

Hence, peer pressure appears to be a productivity incentive, even when merit moneys are modest or unavailable. People will take action in order to sustain the esteem of their colleagues that they would never take on their own or as a result of a supervisor's request.

Customer Satisfaction

Customer satisfaction measures are an excellent way to assess behavior change. Walter Tornow at the Center for Creative Leadership has published work that shows a relationship between high customer satisfaction and productivity in a bank setting. When baseline and successive customer satisfaction measures improve, something positive is happening in the organization.

At Chemetals in Baltimore, salespeople finish client calls with a flourish. The salesperson's last action is to leave the client with a computer disk. The client completes the 360° feedback survey on disk and mails it to a third party for scoring. If the client does not have access to a computer, the salesperson leaves a notebook computer and the survey disk with the client for few minutes. The customer satisfaction measures shown in Figure 9-9 are a result of sequential survey responses by customers for July 1993, December 1993, and July 1994 for Chemetals. Most of these measures of customer satisfaction improved from roughly a mean of 7 to roughly a mean of 8.6. Clearly some intervention improved customer satisfaction scores.

The results show that the most substantial change occurred in

Figure 9-9. Customer service ratings at Chemetals.

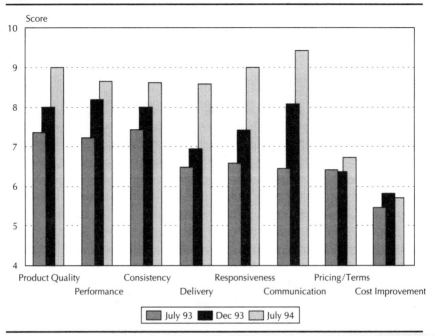

| | July 93 | Dec 93 | July 94 |

communication and perceived salesperson expertise. Responsiveness and delivery increased substantially, and customer satisfaction with overall product quality, overall performance, and product consistency also improved. In contrast, customers saw essentially no difference in this period for pricing/terms or cost improvements. Hence, customer satisfaction improved during a period when Chemetals was not cutting its prices.

Chemetals has been in business a long time. Of course, the change in customer satisfaction probably did not occur solely from the 360° feedback initiative. However, no other training or intervention took place during this period. Since participants think of 360° feedback as a means to improve communication and customer responsiveness, these results are congruent with process experience.

Organizations often use specific productivity indicators to measure facility effectiveness. For example, Figure 9-10 illustrates the baseline customer service indicators of a large communications

Figure 9-10. Customer service impacts at a communications company.

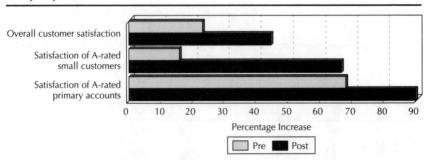

firm where customers respond to a scorecard with ratings of A, B, C, D, or F. One year after the installation of a 360° feedback process, customer service indicators increased substantially: Overall customer satisfaction increased by 100 percent, satisfaction of A-rated small customers by 340 percent, and satisfaction of A-rated primary accounts by 33 percent. The 360° feedback intervention was the only significant organizational change that occurred during this time period at the firm.

360° Feedback and Diversity

Performance measurements drive all human resources systems, including selection, rewards, training and development, and motivation. Hence, the model used for performance measurement has extraordinary impact on all employees' careers. If the performance measurement process discriminates against a specific group, that group will arguably find if not a glass ceiling, then certainly slippery steps up the organizational ladder. Managers should carefully examine the means of measuring performance and seek to use the fairest and most accurate selection method available.

Achievement tests, for example, have repeatedly been shown to be culturally unfair. In fact, some organizations now use *race norming:* different cut-off scores for different ethnic groups to compensate for the well-known adverse impacts on race. Race norming essentially gives members of various races extra credit to make the test equitable. Race norming arose because creators of self-report tests have not figured out how to create achievement tests that are culturally neutral. Similarly, supervisor-only performance measures have been shown to discriminate, probably because no one has figured out how to eliminate bias in individuals. Hence, alternative assessment models should be considered.

Perceived fairness is one of the most significant attributes of 360° feedback systems. However, user perception is not enough. It might, for example, show a preference for 360° feedback even if it was unfair, because it might be "less aversive" or "less unfair" than traditional single-source measures. Diversity fairness examines whether members of minority groups receive performance scores similar to the majority. Of course, an equitable assessment system should pass the test of being fair to all participants—members of groups protected by law and others.

Diversity management addresses the challenge of equitably orchestrating selection decisions, recognition, and rewards independent of age, gender, race, or other factors. Writing and research on diversity management have focused primarily on education, training, and development. Very little has been reported on performance assessment other than research on adverse impacts to protected classes.

Supervisor-only performance measures are more a function of the rater than the ratee. Self-serving, stereotypes, and similar-to-me biases are nearly impossible to train out of supervisors when they rate alone, with no accountability for accuracy. Single-source biases tend to result in lower performance scores for protected classes, such as gender and racial minorities, when the preponderance of supervisors are, probably, white males. When the performance assessment model changes from single-source, supervisor-only evaluation to a multisource process, the performance scores reported in this research change from diversity adverse toward diversity neutral.

The challenge of constantly improving employee behavior requires high-quality and specific performance assessment and feedback, whether or not the feedback is tied to appraisal and pay. An assessment process that produces performance scores with an inappropriately adverse impact on members of diverse groups may create false expectations and false developmental information.

Diversity Fairness Across Three Organizations

An empirical analysis of fairness in performance results examines the data: the performance measurement scores. For each of the three participating organizations in one study, the single-source appraisal systems were found to result in lower performance scores for older performers, women, and people of color. These findings were not surprising because they were consistent with other research on single-source appraisals.

The study also reported 360° feedback scores from the three organizations to see if the performance scores differ significantly for members of groups designated by law as protected status. The data represent the multisource scores of colleagues, direct reports, or both for projects in an industry leader service organization (more than 16,000 employees), an aerospace manufacturer (more than 5,000 employees), and a high-tech communications company (more than 1,300 employees). These sample sizes are so large that even very slight differences in mean performance rating for a group resulted in a statistically significant difference. Therefore, these results should be examined in terms of practical considerations driven by the question: "Given the direction of change in these performance scores, which seems fairer, single-source or multisource assessment systems?" The findings show diversity positive or neutral results that are in direct contrast to the supervisor-only appraisal scores in each of the three organizations.

Age

Results from 360° feedback showed that age and performance were positively correlated for the service organization (Figure 9-11). Age was also slightly positively associated with performance for each of the other two firms. A positive correlation means performance scores increased slightly with age. The data showed that scores rose modestly to age forty-five and then became flat. In these organizations, a move from single-source to multiple source

Figure 9-11. Age and performance scores with 360° feedback at a service company.

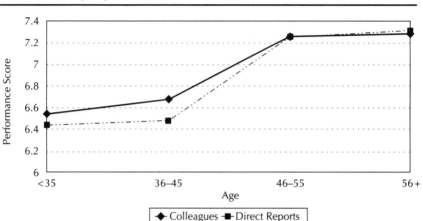

Source: Mark R. Edwards, Ann J. Ewen, and William A. Verdini, "Fair Performance Management and Pay Practices for Diverse Work Forces," *ACA Journal* (Spring 1995).

for performance assessment changed the direction of performance scores for older people from disadvantage to advantage.

Which process is fairer? Certainly for people over forty years old, a 360° feedback process would be preferred.

Gender

The 360° feedback results across all three organizations indicated that women received slightly higher multisource performance scores than men did. The mean scores for men and women from colleagues and direct reports for various organization levels at the service company are shown in Figure 9-12. In this company the difference was positive to women on all thirty-five leadership behaviors. The results from the high-tech communications company were slightly positive to women on 82 percent of the constructs. The aerospace manufacturer resulted higher performance scores for women on twenty-eight of the thirty performance constructs. These gender differences found across these organizations are very small and should be considered neutral.

Why have women met a glass ceiling, limiting their advance

Figure 9-12. Gender and performance scores with 360°
feedback at a service company.

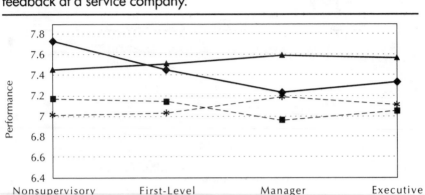

Note: N = 14, 820 for colleagues; N = 6, 789 for direct reports.

Source: Mark R. Edwards, Ann J. Ewen, and William A. Verdini, "Fair Performance Management and Pay Practices for Diverse Work Forces," *ACA Journal* (Spring 1995).

up organization ladders? One reason might be an artifact of the supervisor-only appraisal system. Based on these data, one significant factor associated with the glass ceiling, lower performance scores for women, may be modified by redesigning the appraisal system to use multiple sources.

American Airlines recently won the Catalyst Award for effective use of women in the organization and in management. The award was based, at least partially, on research that showed more equitable scores for women with 360° feedback compared to supervisor-only measures. The use of 360° feedback led to additional policy decisions at American Airlines, such as the creation of a multiple rater, peer selection process as an input for placement and promotion decisions.

People of Color

Demographic data from 360° feedback across these three organizations showed no substantial difference in mean performance

Figure 9-13. People of color and performance scores with 360° feedback at a service company.

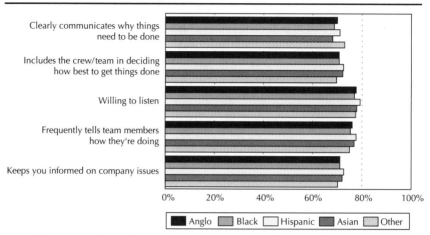

Note: Following are the number of respondents: Anglo, 4,264; black, 372; Hispanic, 340; Asian, 89; other: 18. The total was 5,083.

Source: Mark R. Edwards, "In-Situ Team Evaluation," in *Impact of Leadership,* Kenneth Clark, Miriam Clark, and David Campbell, eds., Center for Creative Leadership, 1992.

scores for Hispanics, blacks, Asians, whites, or others (for the service company, see Figure 9-13). At minimum, these results show people of color were not negatively affected based on 360° feedback performance scores.

Such findings argue that ethnicity fairness is evident in 360° feedback. The data indicate that the multisource assessment appears to create more balanced performance measures that moderate the systemic biases typically found in single-source ratings.

The best approach to performance measurement is yet to be designed, but the data suggest that 360° feedback systems offer substantial improvement to traditional practice in the important area of diversity management.

More research needs to be done on the impact of 360° feedback on performance scores for all people. One encouraging finding is that a recent study at one of the participating organizations indicated that positive age and neutral gender and ethnicity findings have been sustained over three years. Moreover, 360° feedback seems to reverse or neutralize adverse performance scores for members of diversity groups. These results replicate the empirical and anecdotal results from many other 360° feedback projects, among them, at Intel, Hewlett-Packard, the U.S. Department of Energy, IBM, General Electric, General Motors, NCR, Motorola, Public Service Electric & Gas, University of Minnesota, Bausch & Lomb, Humana Hospitals, City of Las Vegas, Consumers' Gas, OXY USA, Federal Express, Florida Power & Light, and TRW.

The Verdict on 360° Feedback

The verdict on 360° feedback remains to be decided. Organizations and researchers will continue to study the impact of 360° feedback. The findings presented in this chapter indicate that 360° feedback has a measurable impact on the fairness of the performance assessment process. It seems to offer an equitable and useful development and assessment process for all organization members.

10

The Future of 360° Feedback

An emerging strategy that offers hope for better economic results, better control of technology, and dignity and meaning too is "getting everybody improving whole systems."

—Marvin R. Weisbord, Principal,
Weisbord, Block & Petrella

Whatever resolves uncertainty is information. Power accrues to whomever can handle information.

—R. Buckminster Fuller

Organizations increasingly will focus on improving productivity. 360° feedback systems act as a catalyst to increasing productivity because feedback from others is the most powerful motivator to behavior change. Innovations in 360° feedback process and software technology will create systems that are more fair, accurate, and valid.

Intelligent systems, which provide knowledge to users on demand or even automatically, will revolutionize human resources decision making. Intelligent systems represent expert knowledge in a manner that serves users. 360° feedback will contribute substantially to intelligent systems by serving as both a tool to collect information and a means of applying it. Intelligence will be integrated into 360° feedback systems in order to make them faster, easier, and better. For example, these systems will not only provide key information about employee performance but will also suggest the best ways to improve it.

Integrated Human Resources Systems

As organizations search for ways of doing more with less, performance measures will be recognized as the key to human productivity. An accurate assessment of an organization's success factors will help it hire new employees who are already strong on its core competencies. Accurate performance measures will correctly target training and development needs and provide a more precise measure of training effectiveness.

Recognition and rewards will have more motivational power because employees will understand that performance, not politics, drives rewards. Accurate measures of success factors will help employees become more effective on those competencies that propel their own success on the job and the organization's productivity. Possibly most important, fair and accurate performance measures mean raises and promotions can go to those who most deserve them.

As additional research supports the accuracy, fairness, and validity of 360° feedback systems, organizations will adopt these systems so they too can gather accurate performance measures. They will be able to use 360° feedback at any time to align individual behaviors with organization values, as well as improve continuous individual, team, and organization learning.

New technology already enables organizations to use online, automated 360° feedback systems at their convenience. This new technology offers the nearly immediate communication of research results, such as validation studies, because the research measures are built into the software. For example, the research methods used to create the diversity effects analysis for 23,000 feedback receivers across three organizations, discussed in Chapter 9, required over 600 research hours. Today, software is available that provides a more comprehensive analysis almost immediately. Organizations like OXY USA, Intel, Tenneco, and Samaritan Health System can examine impacts on diversity or any other demographic or job variable in minutes, at the same time 360° feedback reports are created.

The promise of 360° feedback systems includes their integration with other human resources processes (Figure 10-1). The 360°

Figure 10-1. Integrating strategic human resources decision processes.

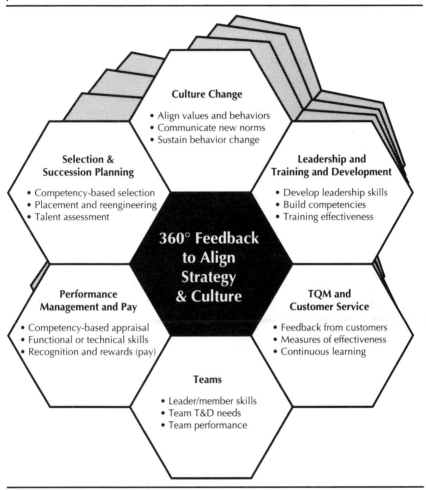

Culture Change
- Align values and behaviors
- Communicate new norms
- Sustain behavior change

Selection & Succession Planning
- Competency-based selection
- Placement and reengineering
- Talent assessment

Leadership and Training and Development
- Develop leadership skills
- Build competencies
- Training effectiveness

360° Feedback to Align Strategy & Culture

Performance Management and Pay
- Competency-based appraisal
- Functional or technical skills
- Recognition and rewards (pay)

TQM and Customer Service
- Feedback from customers
- Measures of effectiveness
- Continuous learning

Teams
- Leader/member skills
- Team T&D needs
- Team performance

feedback process will serve as a linking pin for fairer and more accurate employee and organization decisions. For example, cultural change will be driven by targeted organization competencies, communicated, and assessed using the 360° feedback system. The core competencies or success factors for future leadership will be reflected in the 360° feedback surveys and will spur the development and continuing growth of employees and their leaders.

Once users have firsthand experience with behavior feedback for a culture change process, they will want to use it as well to support leadership, training, and development. Customer service actions will become more integrated into the core competencies as users expand their circle of feedback to encompass external customers. Similarly, teams will be supported with high-quality assessment information from upstream and downstream customers. Team members will receive feedback from team members at any time it is needed.

Naturally, if a new assessment process is more accurate and fairer, users will want it to be extended to support performance appraisal and pay policies. When managers recognize the 360° assessments provide reliable information, they will begin using the results to support selection, placement, and succession planning. 360° feedback serves as an integrator to human resources decision processes because higher-quality assessment information naturally replaces lower-quality information.

A significant part of the promise of 360° feedback systems lies in what will happen in the next generation of intelligent systems. The elements of these intelligent systems are already being field-tested in some organizations.

Intelligent Systems

Traditional assessment systems are passive in the sense that they simply collect data and represent the information in standard reports. Intelligent assessment systems are active in the sense that they will be interactive; those who provide feedback will also ask questions, create scenarios, or even respond to case example. They will coach respondents on how to improve the fairness and accuracy of the data they report by challenging responses that may be invalid because do not meet scientific parameters for consistency with other assessments. These systems may also apply the intelligence built into them to represent and report critical information, such as which competencies best explain performance success for targeted jobs or roles.

Intelligent systems, also called *learning models,* will learn from experience and modify the information they collect based on which serves to predict performance effectiveness best. For example, when a learning system finds certain factors are largely responsible for employee effectiveness, those competencies will be emphasized in assessment and development. These learning models will focus on what counts rather than a wide spectrum of standard competencies.

Intelligent decision systems offer rich opportunities. The 360° feedback model will become a central element for intelligent systems by serving as the:

- Device that extracts the required information. For example, a 360° feedback system that assesses targeted competencies can be customized to measure automatically the behavioral impacts of training and development.
- Model that provides built-in intelligence to evaluate the context of each situation. For example, the 360° feedback system that gathers intelligence is customized to make training and development action recommendations for participants.

Artificial intelligence, expert systems, and decision support procedures can improve human productivity. The following examples offer a glimpse into the intelligent decision systems of the future.

Career Development

Glaxo developed a wide-range career development support system that meshes with the 360° feedback process to assist employees in career development and planning. The process provides career development diagnostics and organization support systems to give employees information on developmental growth needed for building successful careers.

Public Service Electric and Gas in New Jersey segmented the 360° feedback process into five levels based on job families and targeted for the specific values of each group. The career development materials for executive groups are assembled and presented for each specific target audience. The clerical assessment survey, while reflecting the organization's vision and values, uses substantially different terminology from the executive survey for assessing competencies.

The next generation of systems will do more than create customized 360° feedback based on competencies; it will also make recommendations for action. The 360° feedback survey also may be customized to identify behaviors more specifically that represent the best return on investment for employee actions.

Leadership and Employee Development

Most organizations initiate 360° feedback with the intent of strengthening leadership and employee development. American Airlines, the University of Minnesota, Intel, the Department of Energy, GMAC, Motorola, and other users have built multiple levels of intelligence into their leadership development processes. These innovations include the following:

- *Individual intelligence.* Each employee receives behavior feedback in a manner that maximizes understanding and encourages the employee to take steps to improve his or her performance.
- *Employee intelligence.* Each participant is encouraged to discuss developmental feedback with coworkers, who can provide insights that may not be available formally. These discussions essentially fill in the gaps regarding the reasons behind various scores and provide insight as to how others believe performance may be improved.
- *Organization intelligence.* The organization's leadership support systems, which may include specialized training and development, targeted communications, interactive learning, and other developmental opportunities, are available to support targeted leadership development.

Action Recommendations

Some organizations provide employees with recommendations for career development, leadership development, or other performance improvement actions. These processes, still in their infancy, tend to read like paragraphs pulled from a leadership textbook. Other organizations support development plans with materials that itemize developmental actions for a wide variety of behavioral areas. Organizations such as Hallmark Cards, AT&T, and Consumers Gas in Toronto have developed competency dictionaries that describe a wide variety of competencies and also may include ideas for competency development.

Future assessments will provide very specific recommendations for each employee. The recommendations may match the employee's desired career path and set out the competencies for that path, relative to the employee's existing skills. The assessment could thus show employees the gaps between where they are now and where they need to be.

Another approach will recommend actions oriented toward learning from experience and avoiding career derailment. The derailment approach does not tell people how to move ahead in their careers; rather, it tells them how to avoid falling off the career track. Avoiding failure may come from focusing on specific behaviors inferred from an intelligent system.

The 360° feedback process provides a mechanism for collecting and representing targeted intelligence. For example, an automated career development process requires the creation of practical career paths. The 360° feedback process may create the high-quality performance and skill measures that can be used to differentiate behavior profiles that tend to succeed in various career paths. The 360° feedback process may be used to gather and report information across many organization members regarding a number of factors:

- The relative importance of behaviors and skills employed with each job and job family
- The critical competencies needed to succeed in various functional areas
- The highest impact actions when employed with development of selected behaviors or skills
- Leverage points, where targeted actions may improve behavior feedback in several areas
- Practical developmental plans for addressing development opportunities
- Complementary behavior, skills, management style, or personality factors for selection decisions for individuals and teams

Selection and Promotion Systems

Some organizations, including RCA, IBM, Florida Power and Light, Nestlé, and Xerox, have created selection systems based on information captured from multiple sources. Since the 360° feedback information acts as an in-place assessment center, the competency-based assessment information provides highly predictive information on employees. When there is a job opening and employees are nominated, part of the selection process includes the development of a standard or job-specific 360° feedback profile so the most appropriate candidate can be selected. This does not mean that the successful candidate is the one with the highest overall scores. Often it is the shape of the competency profile— the specific strengths an individual brings to a particular job—that serves as the best determinate for selection.

Unlike an assessment center, where cost constrains the organization to limit participation to a small number of candidates, the 360° feedback process involves all employees. Also unlike the assessment center, which occurs only once or twice in an employee's career, the 360° feedback process creates longitudinal information that may provide one or two sets of competency measures each year. Tracking the 360° feedback scores over time yields a highly predictive picture of employees' career development and provides high-quality information for positioning an employee in succession plans.

Some organizations use a behavior or competency-based interview process for job applicants. For example, American Express, America West Airlines, and Samaritan Health System develop job competency profiles for new jobs. Employees interview candidates using structured interview questions designed to elicit information on critical job competencies. Some organizations use the combined insight from the multiple interviewers to improve the quality of information about applicants. The 360° feedback system then creates a documented and systematic method for selecting among the applicants. In the future, intelligent systems will coach interviewers to help them select the best candidate based on competencies. Of course, intelligent systems offer the distinct probability that the interviewer will be the PC rather than a person.

Reengineering and Redeployment

Reengineering redefines the structure and methods of organizations by challenging how things are done. The changes brought about by redesigning work activities often lead to the need to reposition people in new roles.

Prior to reorganizing, ITT-Courier employees reviewed various organization structural options and provided their evaluations to leadership. In addition, they developed a set of core competencies critical to the organization and then profiled existing jobs. When the organization was reengineered, new jobs were profiled based on the critical competencies. Both before and after the reduction in force, employees were assessed on the core competencies. The 360° feedback assessments provided important information for placing employees in the "best-fit" new role. Based on their demonstrated competencies, employees were matched to the roles their competency combination best fit. Although the profile matching at ITT-Courier was not automated, this is an excellent application for intelligent systems.

Assessment Systems

Assessment systems that use the 360° feedback process may have intelligence built in to track and evaluate specific targeted variables, such as ethnicity, age, gender, and other tests of fairness. For example, an organizational policy may require that guidelines for procedural equity be used for all selection decisions, such as training opportunities, opportunities to work on special projects, temporary duty assignments, and the more obvious issues of pay and promotion.

Current 360° feedback processes are passive and allow individual respondents to make assessment judgments based on their own perception. Assessment information may be built into the response system, especially in electronic responses tied into a network. In this environment, respondents can see the entire construct they are evaluating on a computer monitor, defined with illustrative behaviors. Respondents with special needs, such as those for whom English is a second language, may press a key and see the survey in their primary language.

Future changes include building active intelligence into the response systems, such as informing respondents immediately when their judgments are:

- Demonstrating friendship, competition, or other obvious biases
- Showing no distinction across items
- Systematically high or low for various individuals or for protected-status or other groups
- Substantially inconsistent with other respondents

Additional information may coach respondents when they appear to be inadvertently using a different part of the scale (extremely high or low) from other respondents. For example, this action corrects the occasional person who uses the scale backward. Although research indicates that highly discrepant response patterns are unusual, only a few unreliable respondents potentially create significant distortion to the assessment model. Without correction, these few unreliable respondents are likely to increase, which will undermine the integrity of the entire assessment system.

Measurement Precision

Performance assessment systems being refined at du Pont, British Columbia Institute of Technology, and the University of Minnesota are testing intelligence technologies built into 360° feedback. For example, intelligence built into the measurement system can spot measurement unreliability. This characteristic is critical for making decisions about assessment information when used along with traditional information for selection decisions.

Similar intelligence has been used at Current, Inc., Pima County, and Chase Bank to spot construct (question) variance or other sources of error, such as extremely low or high ratings on specific evaluative criteria. Therefore, employees will have better knowledge about the reliability of their performance measures. These measures of information quality are designed to yield high confidence in the measurement process.

Preemployment Profiling

Since 1983, students at Arizona State University have created pre-employment profiles as a supplement to resumés in employment interviews. Classmates, and if possible coworkers, assess the students on competencies and skills that are critical employer needs. While preemployment profiles are more inflated than 360° feedback assessments in a work setting, they do show relative strengths and developmental areas for each candidate. In addition, they provide rich discussion material for employment interviews.

In the future, organizations will use their own core competencies or success factors for profiling potential new hires. For example, job candidates may be asked to provide names and addresses of six people who know their work behaviors. Like an automated reference check, the behavior assessment surveys will be sent to the candidate's evaluation team, along with information on the 360° feedback process and the assurance of response anonymity in return for their cooperation. The organization will gain substantial information regarding these job candidates.

Intelligent systems offer the possibility of looking across a wide variety of candidates to identify candidate skills that match certain job competency profiles. Such systems offer the capacity to go far beyond the single job candidate or single job search that has traditionally been so laborious and time-consuming. In addition, the automated documentation, resulting in the competency profile, represents intelligence that has a long, useful life. Hence, the organization can recall an applicant months later when another job opens. The 360° feedback assessment and storage of competency profiles, along with resumés, could occur on the Internet or other electronic communication services.

Team Building

A base of work styles and competencies important to work groups or teams can be developed from 360° feedback systems. As research and experience clarify which work styles or balances of competencies operate best on a specific team, team membership can be optimized. Intelligent 360° assessment systems will be able to provide targeted assessment and development information that support team leaders and team members.

Succession Planning

Managing internal succession depends on having reliable measures of talent and promotability. Future succession systems will automatically create lists of candidates for specific jobs based on their competency profiles. Automated intelligence systems using experiential information may also create probability statements for the likelihood of success for various selection or placement alternatives. Predicting success will be derived from improvements in measures of success factors required in new jobs, degree of job fit between job requirements and employees, and estimates of required learning time. These systems also may recommend a market-based salary for the combination of competencies the candidate brings to the job. As this type of analysis becomes more refined, the process may actually create alternative scenarios for variations in staffing by modifying position requirements as well as placing people in the best-fit job or role.

Integrity Testing

In the mid-1970s, a major West Coast bank used a multisource process for executive selection. The results were surprising when the heir apparent was evaluated very high by his boss but very low by his colleagues, especially on dependability. The bank president was furious and assumed that the 360° feedback process was incorrect because the results were so different from his expectations. He ordered a complete audit of the process, including verification of all appropriate assessment forms; it verified the integrity of the 360° feedback process.

Several weeks later, the executive who had received the low scores was in the news: he was reported to have absconded with well over $1 million of the bank's money to Mexico, where he promptly disappeared. A focus group of the other bank executives that followed the incident indicated that no one knew of this person's scheme to defraud the bank. His supervisor was largely ignorant of the behavioral indicators. Employees who were colleagues and had rated him, though, apparently observed behaviors that indicated potential problems and gave him relatively low ratings on key behaviors, especially dependability.

Intelligent systems can be built that learn from experience. For example, when an honesty problem occurs, that person's competency profile can be stored and compared with others. As an organization builds knowledge based on competency effectiveness, it can build knowledge based on which competencies are most sensitive to honesty or dishonesty. Such systems have high value in public service jobs or in roles that have an impact on public safety, such as pilots, drivers, or people who handle dangerous cargo. The same method offers solutions for safety, security, and accident avoidance.

The Promise Ahead

Intelligent systems are being developed that can substantially improve career development, measurements of training effectiveness, and the identification of employee problems such as the need for referral to an employee assistance program. Similar intelligent systems offer other enhancements, such as feedback about security or safety.

Future performance measures will create a more self-directed workforce. Employees will begin to expect high-quality and nearly continuous performance measures similar to the market research and sales reports that tell organizations how they are doing in the marketplace. Employees will be receiving information from their internal and external customers—the colleagues with whom they work collaboratively and depend on for organization and career growth and success.

Future intelligent 360° feedback performance measures create a win-win-win situation. Employees win because the information they receive is fair, accurate, and credible. Managers win because their evaluative burden is eased and they are better able to serve as performance coaches. The organization wins because decisions about leadership are more valid and defensible. In addition, intelligent decision systems offer rich opportunities for higher-quality recognition systems because rewards will be directly related to performance, thus improving motivation and productivity.

Positive user experiences and published research will speed the adoption of this new model. The promise of 360° feedback systems is ahead. This will lead more people to understand the insight written by the poet Robert Burns in 1785: *"Oh what a great gift we would have / if we could only see ourselves as others see us."*

Appendix: Sample Competency Assessments for 360° Feedback

Administrative and Organization Skills

Administration and Paperwork
Performs day-to-day paperwork in a timely and accurate manner. Keeps accurate records; administers policies appropriately.

Collecting and Interpreting Data
Interprets numerical data and other relevant information to solve problems, thus facilitating correct inferences; effectively organizes data to help solve problems and make decisions.

Communicating Effectively
Communicates orally and in written form. Obtains and then passes on information to appropriate individuals.

Coordinating and Controlling Resource
Utilizes, coordinates, and balances personnel and other resources to increase unit and organization effectiveness. Controls, monitors, and oversees costs and personnel resources.

Courtesy/Service Support
Demonstrates consideration, cooperation, and generosity in providing service. Shows sensitivity and mobilizes actions to serve customers inside and outside the organization effectively.

Creativity and Innovation

Demonstrates willingness to initiate novel ideas and problem solutions. Reinforcing to others' ideas. Consistently looks for better ways of doing things.

Guiding and Motivating

Provides self-initiative and direction, with recognition, encouragement, constructive criticism, and other feedback. Sets and monitors performance goals for self and subordinates.

Handling Crisis and Stress

Recognizes and responds effectively to unexpected situations; handles crises and stress calmly and effectively; responds to tight time deadlines; addresses conflict appropriately.

Interpersonal Skills

Develops and maintains smooth and effective working relationships with superiors and coworkers; displays personal concern for others; encourages and fosters cooperation between subordinates.

Leadership

Guides, directs, and positively affects the actions and results of individuals and groups; motivates; initiates dialogue with subordinates.

Organization Skills

Works effectively within the framework of the organization's policies, procedures, rules, and goals; carries out orders and directives; supports reasonable policies of organization.

Persistence in Reaching Goals

Persists with extra effort to attain objectives; overcomes obstacles to get the job done.

Planning and Organizing

Formulates short- and long-term goals and objectives; forecasts possible problems and develops strategies for addressing these problems; organizes and prioritizes work; time management.

Problem Analysis/Decision Making

Makes sound and timely decisions; takes into account all relevant information in making decisions; develops effective solutions to organization problems.

Professional and Technical Proficiency

Keeps up to date technically; possesses sufficient technical job knowledge to perform effectively in own specialty; provides technical advice to others in the organization.

Career Development

Guiding and Motivating
Guides, directs, and motivates subordinates.

Technical Proficiency
Keeps up to date technically and solves technical problems within the organization.

Administration and Paperwork
Handles administrative and paperwork requirements effectively and in a timely manner.

Handling Crisis and Stress
Recognizes and responds effectively to unexpected situations.

Meeting Commitments
Sets appropriate priorities to accomplish planned projects on time.

Team Contributor
Works well as part of a team; systematically encourages and supports others.

Work Perspective
Maintains positive enthusiasm toward job accountabilities and objectives.

Quality of Work
Meets challenges and overcomes adversity while maintaining high standards of quality.

Decision Making
Assembles facts, considers alternatives, and balances competing considerations before reaching sound conclusions.

Innovation/Problem Solving
Understands legitimate needs and diagnoses problems.

Organization and Planning
Anticipates obstacles and contingencies and allocates resources to meet changing needs.

Communication Skills
Demonstrates effective verbal and written skills in individual and group settings.

Advancement Potential
Demonstrates willingness and ability to learn and grow personally and professionally.

Professional Accountability
Very professional; customers and work associates can rely on performance.

Challenging the Process
Recognizes good ideas, supports them, and challenges the system to get new ideas adopted.

Organization Climate

Encouragement
To what extent are you encouraged to develop new ways to do your job?

Decision Making
To what extent are you allowed to make decisions to improve the way you perform your job?

Additional Effort
To what extent are you willing to put forth additional effort to increase your contribution?

Solving Problems
To what extent are you and your coworkers effective at solving problems together?

Creativity
To what extent are people encouraged to be creative in their jobs?

Recognition
To what extent are individual accomplishments and contributions recognized?

Poor Performance
To what extent is poor performance dealt with effectively?

Information
To what extent are you satisfied with the amount of information you receive?

Business Decisions
To what extent do you receive an adequate amount of information about reasons behind business decisions?

Input on Suggestions
To what extent do you have the opportunity to express your suggestions regarding departmental policies and procedures?

Organizational Awareness
To what extent are you sufficiently aware of things happening that might affect how you do your job?

Operational Efficiency
To what extent do we operate efficiently?

Decision Levels
To what extent are decisions made by employees at the appropriate level?

Independent Action
To what extent are people at your level free to take independent actions that are necessary to carry out their responsibilities?

Overall Change
To what extent do we seem to be changing for the better?

Communication Skills

Listens
Listens attentively to others when they speak.

Doesn't Interrupt
Does not interrupt when others are talking.

Eye Contact
Faces and maintains eye contact with those who are speaking.

Asks Questions
Asks questions when he or she doesn't understand what someone is saying.

Speaks Clearly
Speaks in a clear voice.

Asks Verification Questions
Asks other questions to make sure he or she understands what has been said.

Understandable
Uses words and terms that others can understand.

Empathetic
Puts herself or himself in others' shoes and understands the feelings and motivations of others.

Written Communication
Has effective written and oral communication.

Pace
Speaks at a reasonable rate.

Voice
Uses understandable tone and enunciation.

Public Presentation
Presents effectively before groups.

Group Effectiveness

Roles of Members
Ensures that the members' specialized skills are identified and that each person makes a useful contribution.

Appropriate Structure
Takes initiatives to organize the group in ways that are suitable to the task.

Conscious of Methods
Observes the way the group operates so that any immaturity or problems can be acknowledged and discussed.

Acts as a Sieve
Puts ideas in sequence, helping the group keep on track, and scheduling business so that items are dealt with in an orderly fashion.

Clarifies Contributions
Checks on whether contributions are understood and ensures that any areas of uncertainty are clarified.

Asks for Ideas/Reactions
Encourages people to express their views, suggestions, and reactions—especially people who appear withdrawn.

Gives Airtime
Takes definite action to ensure that everyone's viewpoint is fully heard.

Maintains Discipline
Draws attention to behavior that is undermining group effectiveness.

Resource Utilization
Draws attention to available resources and assists in their introduction.

Clear Objectives
Creates clear objectives and precise tasks. Evaluates contributions regularly.

Support
Supports group with open communication, material support, and company-wide acceptance.

Coordinated Activity
Coordinates individual activities to support independent yet aligned initiatives.

Heart
Uplifts the spirits of the group when snags and setbacks occur, so that challenges do not demoralize the group's initiative and energy.

Communication Effectiveness
Communicates necessary information without giving data overload. Identifies and discusses key topics.

Process Review
Guidelines are updated as new data are generated; tasks are changed to incorporate the changes in character and scope.

Customer Service Proficiencies

Application
Applies problem-solving process.

Available
Is available and does what's needed to solve problems.

Communication
Listens and communicates effectively.

Company Knowledge
Knows company and customer business/products.

Constant Improvement
Continues self-development.

Contact for Support
Knows who, what, when, and where to contact for support.

Foresight
Predicts problems and takes action.

Handles Stress
Deals effectively with pressure and emotions of other individuals.

Informative
Keeps people abreast on current issues.

Knows Subject
Proficient and knowledgeable of subject.

Patient
Tolerates dilemmas of service role.

Team Building
Involves others.

Understands Needs
Understands customer needs and expectations.

Understands Personalities
Understands customer and company personalities.

Up to Date
Keeps up to date on competition.

Effective Coaching

Approachable
Easy to approach and talk with.

Fair
Deals fairly with his or her team members.

Honest
Honest with team members.

Dependable
Keeps promises.

Respect
Kind to team members and treats each one with respect.

Loyal
Loyal to others—doesn't say something to one's face and something else behind one's back.

Uses Apologies
Apologizes to team members when it is appropriate.

Honors Expectations
Honors the expectations of others; realizes that we don't all see things the same way.

Involves Team Members
Involves team members in setting performance goals and objectives.

Provides Information
Provides the information necessary for team members to achieve their goals.

Provides Resources
Provides the resources necessary for team members to achieve their goals.

Provides Performance Feedback
Provides frequent performance feedback to team members.

Provides Accurate Feedback
Provides accurate feedback to team members.

Praises Team Members
Praises team members regularly for good performance/behavior.

Recognizes and Rewards
Reinforces team members' good performance with appropriate rewards.

Effective Teams

Quality and Accountability
Group produces high-quality work and takes responsibility for its product and actions.

Listens to Users
Obtains information from the users of the group's projects to channel the group's progress more profitably.

Innovative Spirit
Demonstrates ability to devise new or improved methods to get the job done.

Communication Across Department
Supplies necessary departments with clear and concise information about the current progress/status.

Bias for Action
Motivates group to achieve goals in a timely manner. Healthy impatience; keeps group moving forward.

Participative Decisions
Reaches decisions through joint measures; utilizes all resources and inputs of the group.

Equitable Rewards
Demonstrates that the result is worth the time spent.

Teamwork Encouraged
Encourages group participation and achievement of a common goal. Demonstrates constructive, supportive interaction and the constant development of group cohesiveness.

Develops People
Demonstrates that participation in the group improves individual performance.

Matches Skills/Tasks
Utilizes group members in the areas where their greatest contribution can be made. Tasks commensurate with abilities.

Coaching and Support
Demonstrates attentiveness and interest through verbal and nonverbal means.

Customer Service
Achieves, improves, and attains customer service results. Focuses on customer.

Trust/Shared Purpose
Demonstrates a defined common goal, and all members show a commitment to that purpose/goal.

Enthusiasm and Pride
Displays a continued interest and enthusiasm for group goal.

Objectivity
Discusses and evaluates problems without involving individual emotions. Demonstrates realistic ideas about what is good for the group as a whole.

Leadership

Benchmarks
Monitors the department's progress through competitive benchmark-

ing. Compares the department with other similar internal/external operations to ensure it's the best it can be.

Shows Initiative
Is always looking for a better way to get the job done and willing to try new things.

Visionary
Sees the big picture; knows how their job and department affects the organization. Does not see everything from a local perspective.

Involves Others
Includes team members from inside and, where appropriate, outside the station/department when deciding how best to get the job done. Is a good problem solver.

Communicates
Is a good, active listener and asks questions to ensure understanding. Does not constantly interrupt. Does not display an "I know what's right" attitude.

Supports Teamwork
Encourages people to work together as a team to solve common problems. Inspires; creates excitement so team members want to work harder and perform well. Encourages interdepartmental teamwork.

Anticipates Problems
Always looks ahead and identifies problems before they occur. Takes appropriate action to mitigate/resolve problems while they are small.

Takes Action
Makes an effort to locate and remove barriers that reduce efficiency.

Commits to Leadership
Leadership style treats this commitment as a basic business principle.

Delegates Effectively
Encourages and supports others to take on added responsibility, authority, and accountability.

Supports Others
Encourages individuals to monitor their own efforts. Acts as a resource and coach in allowing individuals to reach their full potential.

Clarifies Expectations
Lets people know what is expected of them. Sets clear levels of expectation based on mutually agreed upon goals.

Acts as Role Model
Leads by example; good role model for the team. Does not say one thing and do another.

Recognizes Performance
Recognizes people for doing a good job.

Demonstrates Organization
Ensures regularly scheduled reviews of progress toward goals. Sets appropriate priorities to accomplish planned projects on time.

Negotiation Skills

Establishes Desired Results
Establishes her or his own desired results before negotiating begins.

Is Prepared
Comes prepared with relevant information for negotiating.

Seeks Understanding
Seeks a clear understanding of the situation before and during negotiations.

Seeks Win-Win Situations
Works toward win-win outcomes; all parties get what they want.

Understands Others
Strives to understand others before seeking to be understood.

Seeks Best Solution
Strives for best possible solution, regardless of personal desires.

Peak Performance

Inherent Talent
Exhibits an inborn predisposition to specific talents.

Acquired Information
Recalls and appropriately uses a mass of learned skills and data about the world.

Restlessness
Displays an inner urge to apply talent and information.

Passion and Preference
Demonstrates an intense commitment to own tasks and activities.

A Sense of Mission
Portrays an image of the desired state of affairs that inspires action, determines behavior, and fuels motivation.

Results
Achieves results and measurable goals within set time frames. Demonstrates no fear of failure.

Cultivates Necessary Skills
Acquires new skills that will serve the mission. Seeks new information. Emphasizes growth training.

Learned Effectiveness
Separates action that produces useful results in real time from mere activity or busy work. Works smart.

Collaborator
Attracts other people and their resources to organization/unit projects by use of a magnet mentality. Builds teams.

Self-Manager
Sees oneself as the originator of actions in one's life. Views events as opportunities for taking action.

Self-Mastery
Orchestrates and develops personal mental and emotional strengths. Demonstrates self-confidence. Sees both the viewpoint of the company and the viewpoint of own department.

Team Building/Team Playing
Gains leverage by empowering others to produce. Stretches the abilities of others. Encourages educated risk taking.

Course Correction
Stays on the critical pathway to goal. Utilizes mental agility and concentration and learns from mistakes.

Change Management
Sees change as a source of opportunity he or she can guide, not as something to resist. Anticipates and adapts.

Safety Behaviors

Acts Practically
Does things in a reasonable fashion.

Aware of Surroundings
Demonstrates sensitivity to the situation, the total environment.

Follows the Rules
Does not try to short-cut safe procedures.

Knows Personal Skills
Demonstrates accurate self-perception regarding strengths and weaknesses.

Deploys Personal Skills
Uses personal skills effectively.

Promotes Safety
Makes people feel that what they do has meaning and significance in regard to the success of the organization and in regard to safe working conditions.

Personally Accountable
Demonstrates ability to be counted on to do what he or she says will be done.

Handles Crisis and Stress
Responds effectively to challenges, deadlines, and emergencies.

Energizes Others
Uses a "pull" style of influence that attracts and energizes people toward the goal of safe working conditions.

Does Things Well
Demonstrates an efficient manner but not so fast as to be unsafe.

Does the Right Things
Focuses effort on what counts the most.

Avoids Problems
Anticipates and avoids problems. Does not have to constantly fight fires because crises are avoided.

Emotionally Stable
Displays a constancy in personal behavior.

Demonstrates Creativity and Innovation
Demonstrates a willingness to initiate novel ideas and problem solutions. Portrays an open and reinforcing attitude to others' ideas. Consistently looks for better ways of doing things.

Challenges the Assumptions
Shows a willingness to challenge the rules if they are obsolete, unsafe, or inappropriate for the circumstance.

Recommended Reading

Bader, Gloria E., and Audrey E. Bloom. "How to Do a Peer Review." *Training and Development* 46 (6) (June 1992): 61–66.

Bayroff, A. G., et al. "Validity of Ratings as Related to Rating Techniques and Conditions." *Personnel Psychology* 7 (1954): 93–114.

Bedeian, Arthur G. "Rater Characteristics Affecting the Validity of Performance Appraisals." *Journal of Management* 2 (1976): 37–45.

Berkshire, J. R., and P. D. Nelson. "Leadership Peer Rating Related to Subsequent Proficiency in Training and in the Fleet." Special Report 58–20. Pensacola, Fla.: Naval School of Aviation Medicine, 1958.

Bernardin, H. J. "Subordinate Appraisal: A Valuable Source of Information About Managers." *Human Resource Management* 25 (1986): 421–439.

Bernardin, H. J., and E. C. Pence. "Effects of Rater Training: Creating New Response Sets and Decreasing Accuracy." *Journal of Applied Psychology* (1980): 60–66.

Bland, Carole J., Mark R. Edwards, and Leonard V. Kuhi. "Academic Administrator Evaluation Through Colleague Feedback." *CUPA Journal* 45 (1) (Spring 1994): 19–31.

Booker, G. S., and R. W. Miller. "A Closer Look at Peer Ratings." *Personnel* 43 (1966): 42–47.

Borman, W. C. "Format and Training Effects on Rating Accuracy and Rater Errors." *Journal of Applied Psychology* 64 (1979): 410–421.

———. "Exploring Upper Limits of Reliability and Validity in Performance Ratings." *Journal of Applied Psychology* 63 (1978): 135–144.

Bowman, James S. "At Last an Alternative to Performance Appraisal: Total Quality Management." *Public Administration Review* 54 (2) (March–April 1994): 129–136.

Bretz Jr., Robert D., G. T. Milkovich, and Walter Read. "The Current State of Performance Appraisal Research and Practice: Concerns, Directions, and Implications." *Journal of Management* 8 (1992): 321–352.

Deming, W. E. 1986. *Out of the Crisis.* Cambridge: MIT, Center for Advanced Engineering Study.

Dorfman, Peter W., Walter G. Stephan, and John Leveland. "Performance Appraisal Behaviors: Supervisor Perceptions and Subordinate Reactions." *Personnel Psychology* 39 (Autumn 1986): 579–597.

Downey, R. G., et al. "Evaluation of Peer Rating Systems for Preduty Subsequent Promotion of Senior Military Officers." *Journal of Applied Psychology* 61 (2) (1976): 206–209.

Edwards, Mark R. "Symbiotic Leadership: A Creative Partnership for Managing Organizational Effectiveness." *Business Horizons* (May–June 1992): 28–33.

————. "In-Situ Team Evaluation: A New Paradigm for Measuring and Developing Leadership at Work." In Kenneth E. Clark, Miriam B. Clark, and David P. Campbell, eds., *Impact of Leadership.* Greensboro, N.C.: Center for Creative Leadership, 1992.

————. "Accurate Performance Measurement Tools." *HRMagazine* (June 1991): 95–98.

————. "Assessment: Implementation Strategies, Multirater Systems." *Personnel Journal* (September 1990): 130–139.

————. "Turning the Appraisals Tables." *Information Strategy: The Executive's Journal* (Summer 1990): 31–34.

————. "Assessment: A Joint Effort Leads to Accurate Appraisals." *Personnel Journal* (June 1990): 122–128.

————. "An Alternative to Traditional Appraisal Systems." *Supervisory Management* (June 1990).

————. "Changing Fiefdoms to Contributors with Multisource Assessment." In Richard Bellingham, ed., *The Corporate Culture Sourcebook.* Boston: HRD Press, 1990.

————. "Sustaining Culture Change with Multiple-Rater Systems for Career Development and Performance Appraisal Systems." *Corporate Culture Sourcebook* (1990): 194–205.

————. "Making Performance Appraisals Meaningful and Fair." *Business* (July–September 1989): 17–22.

————. "Artificial Intelligence: Building New HR Productivity Solutions." *HR/PC* (January–February 1989): 10–15.

————. "Measuring Creativity at Work: Developing a Reward-for-Creativity Policy." *Journal of Creative Behavior* 23 (1) (1989): 26–37.

————. "An Expert System for Equitable Career Decisions" *Computers in Personnel* (Fall 1988): 40–47.

———. "Confronting Alcoholism Through Team Evaluation." *Business Horizons* 29 (3) (May–June 1986): 78–83.

———. "Team Talent Assessment: Optimizing Assessee Visibility and Assessment Accuracy." *Human Resources Planning* 8 (3) (Fall 1985): 157–171.

———. "Performance Appraisal for Matrix Management." *Journal of the Society of Research Administrators* 17 (1) (Summer 1985): 33–47.

———. "Safeguarding Your Employee Rating System." *Business* 35 (2) (April–June 1985): 17–27.

———. "Making Performance Appraisals Perform: The Use of Team Evaluation." *Personnel* 62 (3) (March 1985): 28–32.

———. "Rating the Raters Improves Performance Appraisals." *Personnel Administrator* 28 (8) (August 1983): 77–83.

———. "Wolf Hunting: Are There Wolves in Your Organization?" *Public Personnel Administration* 3 (1983): 117–127.

———. "Productivity Improvement Through Innovations in Performance Appraisal." *Public Personnel Management Journal* 12 (1) (Spring 1983): 113–124.

Edwards, Mark R., Carol J. Bland, and Leonard V. Kuhi. "Academic Administrator Evaluation Through Colleague Feedback." *CUPA Journal* (Spring 1994): 19–29.

Edwards, Mark R., and Walter C. Borman. "Solving the Double Bind in Performance Appraisal: A Saga of Wolves, Sloths and Eagles." *Business Horizons* 23 (3) (May–June 1985): 59–68.

Edwards, Mark R., and Suzanne H. Cooke. "Comparative Evaluation of the Accuracy of Team and Supervisor-Only Evaluations of Female Job Performance." *International Journal of Management* (December 1988): 400–412.

Edwards, Mark R., and S. Cook. "Why Women Benefit from Multiple Rater Consensus Decision Technology." *Gender and Society* 5 (16) (Spring 1988): 36–43.

Edwards, Mark R., and Leslie J. Cummings. "Appraising Work Group Performance: New Productivity Opportunities in Hospitality Management." *FIU Hospitality Review* 4 (2) (Fall 1986): 20–33.

Edwards, Mark R., and Ann J. Ewen. "The Glass Ceiling: Fact or Artifact?" *Perspectives in Human Resources* (May 1993).

———. "Integrating Fiefdoms Into Organizational Networks." *Review* (February–March 1993): 45–54.

———. "Making Better Performance Easier with Multisource Assessment." *National Society for Performance and Instruction* 34 (2) (February 1995): 20–22.

———. "Moving Multisource Assessment Beyond Development: The Linkage Between 360-Degree Feedback, Performance Appraisal and Pay." *ACA Journal* (Winter 1995): 2–13.

Edwards, Mark R., Ann J. Ewen, and Sandra O'Neal. "Using Multisource Assessment to Pay People, Not Jobs." *ACA Journal* (Summer 1994): 19–29.

Edwards, Mark R., Ann J. Ewen, and William A. Verdini. "Fair Performance Management and Pay Practices for Diverse Work Forces: The Promise of Multisource Assessment." *ACA Journal* (Spring 1995): 50–63.

Edwards, Mark R., and Leonard D. Goodstein. "Experiential Learning Can Improve the Performance Appraisal Process." *Human Resource Management* (Spring 1982): 18–23.

Edwards, Mark R., and William A. Verdini. "Technical Management: Accurate Human Performance Measures = Productivity." *Journal of the Society of Research Administrators* 18 (2) (Fall 1986): 23–37.

Ewen, Ann J. "Multisource Assessment Increases Healthcare Employee Satisfaction." *Journal of AHIMA* 65 (5) (May 1994): 56–60.

———. "Fairness and Performance Appraisal: The Multisource Assessment Process." Ph.D. dissertation. University of Colorado, 1994.

Fay, C. H., and G. P. Latham. "Effects of Training and Rating Scales on Rating Errors." *Personnel Psychology* 35 (Spring 1982): 105–116.

Fiske, D., and J. Cox. "The Consistency of Ratings by Peers." *Journal of Applied Psychology* 44 (1960): 11–17.

George, David I., and Mike C. Smith. "An Empirical Comparison of Self-Assessment and Organizational Assessment in Personnel Selection." *Public Personnel Management* 19 (2) (Summer 1990): 175–190.

Gilliland, Stephen W. "The Perceived Fairness of Selection Systems: An Organizational Justice Perspective." *Academy of Management Review* 18 (4) (1993): 694–734.

Gordon, L. V., and F. F. Medland. "The Cross Group Stability of Peer Ratings of Leadership Potential." *Personnel Psychology* 18 (1965): 173–177.

Greenhaus, Jeffrey H., Saroj Parasuraman, and Wayne J. Wormley. "Effects of Race on Organizational Experiences, Job Performance Evaluations, and Career Outcomes." *Academy of Management Journal* 33 (1) (1990): 64–85.

Harris, Michael M., and John Schaubroeck. "A Meta-Analysis of Self-

Supervisor, Self-Peer, and Peer-Supervisor Ratings." *Personnel Psychology* 41 (1) (Spring 1988): 43–62.

Hartel, Charmine E. J. "Rating Format Research Revisited: Format Effectiveness and Acceptability Depend on Rater Characteristics." *Journal of Applied Psychology* 78 (2) (April 1993): 212–217.

Hegarty, Harvey. "Using Subordinate Ratings to Elicit Behavioral Changes in Supervisors." *Journal of Applied Psychology* 59 (6) (1974): 764–766.

Heneman, Herbert III. "Comparisons of Self and Superior Ratings of Managerial Performance." *Journal of Applied Psychology* 59 (5) (1974): 638–642.

Kane, Jeffrey S., and Edward E. Lawler III. "Methods of Peer Assessment." *Psychological Bulletin* 85 (3) (1978): 555–586.

Kaplan, Robert E. "360-Degree Feedback Plus: Boosting the Power of Co-Worker Ratings for Executives." *Human Resource Management* 32 (2 and 3) (Summer–Fall 1993): 299–314.

Landy, Frank J., Janet L. Barnes, and Kevin R. Murphy. "Correlates of Perceived Fairness and Accuracy of Performance Evaluation." *Journal of Applied Psychology* 63 (6) (1978): 751–754.

Lawler III, Edward E. "The Multitrait-Multirater Approach to Measuring Managerial Job Performance." *Journal of Applied Psychology* 51 (1967): 369–381.

Lewin, A. Y., and A. Zwany. "Peer Nominations: A Model, Literature Critique, and a Paradigm for Research." *Personnel Psychology* 29 (1976): 423–447.

London, Manuel, and Richard W. Beatty. "360-Degree Feedback as a Competitive Advantage." *Human Resource Management* 32 (2 and 3) (Summer–Fall 1993): 353–372.

London, Manuel, and Arthur J. Wohlers. "Agreement between Subordinate and Self-Ratings in Upward Feedback." *Personnel Psychology* 44 (2) (1991).

Mabe, P. A., and S. G. West. "Validity of Self-Evaluation of Ability: A Review and Meta-Analysis." *Journal of Applied Psychology* (67) (1982): 280–296.

McClelland, David C. "Testing for Competence Rather Than for Intelligence." *American Psychologist* (January 1973): 1–14.

McGarvey, Robert, and Scott Smith. "When Workers Rate the Boss." *Training* 30 (3) (March 1993): 31–34.

Norwack, K. M. "360-Degree Feedback: The Whole Story." *Training & Development Journal* (47) (1993): 69–72.

Norwack, K. M. "Self-Assessment and Rater-Assessment as a Dimension of Management Development." *Human Resources Development Quarterly* (3) (1992): 141–155.

Roadman, H. E. "An Industrial Use of Peer Ratings." *Journal of Applied Psychology* (August 1964): 211–213.

Roberson-Saunders, Pat. "Using Feedback to Improve Staff Performance." *Supervisory Management* 36 (8) (August 1991): 3.

Sackett, Paul R., and Cathy L. Z. DuBois. "Rater-Ratee Race Effects on Performance Evaluation: Challenging Meta-Analytic Conclusions." *Journal of Applied Psychology* 76 (6) (December 1991): 873–877.

Schneier, Craig Eric. "Multiple Rater Groups and Performance Appraisal." *Public Personnel Management* (January–February 1977): 13–20.

Tett, R., D. Jackson, and M. Rothstein. "Personality Measures as Predictors of Job Performance: A Meta-Analytic Review." *Personnel Psychology* (44) (1991): 703–742.

Thomas, Roosevelt R., Jr. "From Affirmative Action to Affirming Diversity." *Harvard Business Review* (March–April 1990): 107–117.

Thorton, G. C. "The Relationship between Supervisory and Self Appraisals of Executive Performance." *Personnel Psychology* 21 (1968): 441–445.

Torrow, Walter W., and Jack W. Wiley. "Service Quality and Management Practices: A Look at Employee Attitudes, Customer Satisfaction, and Bottom-Line Consequences." *Human Resource Planning* 14 (2) (1994): 105–115.

Whitla, D. K., and J. E. Tirrell. "The Validity of Ratings of Several Levels of Supervisors." *Personnel Psychology* 6 (1953): 461–466.

Wohlers, Arthur J., and Manuel London. "Ratings of Managerial Characteristics: Evaluation Difficulty, Co-Worker Agreement, and Self-Awareness." *Personnel Psychology* 42 (1989): 235–260.

Index